# Creating Dance
## A Traveler's Guide

Edited by

Carol M. Press

Edward C. Warburton

**HAMPTON PRESS, INC.**
**NEW YORK, NEW YORK**

Library of Congress Cataloging-in-Publication Data

Creating dance : a traveler's guide / edited by Carol M. Press and Edward C. Warburton.
      pages cm
   Includes bibliographical references and index.
   ISBN 978-1-61289-112-5 (hardbound) — ISBN 978-1-61289-113-2 (paperbound)
   1. Dancers—Biography.   2. Dance teachers—Biography.   3. Choreographers—
Biography.   I. Press, Carol M.   II. Warburton, Edward C.
   GV1785.A1C64 2013
   792.802'8092—dc23                                        2012050897

Hampton Press, Inc.
307 Seventh Ave.
New York, NY 10001

# Contents

*To Nicholas, Samantha and Haydn*

# Preface

# ¡Buen Viaje!

## Bill Evans

I met Ted Warburton when he received the Emerging Leader Award at the National Dance Education Organization conference I produced in Albuquerque in 2003. I was impressed by his eloquence on that occasion and even more so when we later served together on the NDEO Board of Directors. At the 2004 NDEO conference in East Lansing, Michigan, I met Carol Press. When she boldly asked me to witness a solo she had choreographed for herself and I freely shared my perceptions, we experienced an immediate bonding. For the Buffalo conference in 2005 we collaborated on a deeply satisfying presentation of our respective choreography and performance. Over the years, I have been inspired by the alacritous ways that Carol and Ted seek collaboration, ask fundamental questions, encourage life-long learning and embrace diversity of thought and action. I have been pleased to consider them friends, and I was doubly pleased to receive the invitation to write a few words about their most recent project.

I love the notion that *creating dance* is different from (but includes) *creating dances*. For me, removing the hierarchy from our art form sheds light on the essential but sometimes minimized value of contributions made by dancers, teachers, scholars, administrators, students, advocates and even parents who enroll their children in dance classes. While reading these engrossing essays, I realized that I often create an internal hierarchy, valuing the part of me that choreographs dances more than the parts that teach students to embody those dances, produce and market the concerts that allow those dances to be performed, and find the money to make those productions possible. Reflecting on this collection has nudged me to reconsider, validate and find deeper satisfaction in the various ways that I and others create dance. Each of these collected stories reminds me that making dances is but one facet of the work that builds an environment where dance survives and matters.

Carol and Ted invited an unexpected selection of people whose existence is centered in dance to tell their unique tales of lived experience. I know some of these writers well, but I was fascinated by the new information, surprising word choices and idiosyncratic points of view revealed in their conversations. I have not met several of these contributors, but after reading their stories I look forward to doing so. They have contextualized their stories from dramatically different perspectives and the Laban movement analyst in me would like to observe those I do not yet know before meeting them to see if I can match their movement signatures to the distinctive qualities revealed in their writings.

How refreshing to be invited into these musings on the meaning of a life devoted to the love of dance. How stimulating to focus on some of our unsung heroes, and to be reminded that most of us who devote our lives to creating dance do not achieve wide recognition or fame. We are driven by the intrinsic satisfactions of making our corners of the world better places by leading embodied lives, overcoming marginalization, celebrating personal voices and unleashing the power of our imaginations. Each of us sees, hears, feels and makes meaning through highly individual lenses. As I read about the thoughts and feelings that propel these diverse dancers on their respective journeys, I became a grateful recipient of their narrative gifts. As I examined the selected and reconstructed details of inner experience that each has organized for this venture I felt less alone and found myself confronting memories and unpacking my own thoughts and feelings about a life devoted to creating dance.

This book motivates me to generate more layers of knowledge about the diversity, psychology and sociology of those who create dance in all its manifestations. I am moved to take a step back and look with fresh eyes at the multifaceted, challenging and enthralling world of dance I have inhabited since childhood. As you read these essays, I invite you to join me in using this traveler's guide to navigate the vast terrains and landscapes of meaning intrinsic to creating dance. ¡Buen viaje!

# Acknowledgments

*Creating Dance: A Traveler's Guide* had a long gestation, and through the support, encouragement, and contributions of key individuals in our lives, has finally come to fruition. We are forever grateful to the president of Hampton Press, Barbara Bernstein, for offering unwavering commitment to us as we explored a number of avenues of thought. We wanted to expand the notion of creating dance, *well put* by Bill Evans in the Preface: "I love the notion that *creating dance* is different from (but includes) *creating dances....* Each of these collected stories reminds me that making dances is but one facet of the work that builds an environment where dance survives and matters." We sought to bring forward voices that have not yet been heard, voices that speak of core endeavors and values in our field. We invited an exceptional selection of people whose lives are centered in dance to tell their tales of lived experiences. The true value of *Creating Dance* is in their perseverance and love of the art form.

Simon Dove's insightful questions, and focused intelligence helped this project take root. Ongoing dialogues with our colleagues at conferences helped us crystallize our direction. Jacqueline Smith-Autard's works on creativity have deepened our understanding of the field. Dancers who are close colleagues—Alice Condodina, Angelia Leung, Christina McCarthy, Christopher Pilafian, Delila Mosely, Ilana Morgan, Mira Kingsley, Nancy Colahan, Ninotchka Bennahum, Tonia Shimin, Valerie Huston, and Vickie Scott—confirm and reinforce our own scholarship and artistry. Crossing disciplines, colleagues in psychology, music, and art—Alan Kindler, Anna Ornstein, George Hagman, Joe Lichtenberg, Julia Schwartz, Karen Schwartz, Leslie Hogan, the late Marion Tolpin, Medford Moreland, Rosalind Chaplin Kindler, and Todd Walker—continually broaden our perspectives.

This project has been deepened by our association with the travelers in this guide, who have expanded the possible terrains for us all. You offer an example of creating dance and creating a life through dance in a vast variety of dynamic spheres. Your experiences provide the bedrock for extending our horizons. True fruition of this project will come as readers engage your worlds, and hopefully find new directions and support for their own. That is what is most important here. That others pay attention to, and evolve through, their own travels as they create dance in whatever fashion is most meaningful to them and their cultures.

Significantly, we want to acknowledge our students. You push our thinking as you express your curiosity of how one maintains and sustains a life in dance. What happens if you are not going to perform with a major company, or do perform, and then wish to continue to contribute to dance? What pathways that might not be traditional or immediately obvious can one look down and find a potential for engagement? In many ways, this volume is a thank you for the gifts you have offered us as teachers.

In addition to Barbara Bernstein, we want to thank editor Robin Weisberg, who worked enthusiastically on the text. Kane Anderson, research assistant extraordinaire, always came to the rescue when work needed to be accomplished. We offer our gratitude to Tom Phon for his cover design, which subtly and beautifully evokes both the anticipation of path and joy of journey. Most importantly, we acknowledge our families without whose patience and support this project would not have been possible. Finally, we thank each other for making the long hours of conversation full of laughter and insight.

## Prologue

# Creating Dance

## Landscapes of Meaning

Carol M. Press
Edward C. Warburton

Creating dance for self and others engages all human beings in all lands who are drawn to moving with aesthetic intention. Such a terrain includes those who transmit dance traditions, participants who bear witness, toddlers who bounce on their parents' knees, artists who envision new ways of world making, presenters who provide performance platforms, instructors who lead, students who move along, flash mobs that improvise in the streets of international festivals, educators who dream creative courses of study, historians who contextualize the past, theorists who envision the future, and institutions that build the foundation on which dance thrives. These lands provide the fertile ground for humanity's need, desire, and love of dance; a journey worth taking!

*Creating Dance: A Traveler's Guide* introduces creating dance as a goal, an activity, and a state of being. Creating dance is lived phenomena in actual places: the landscape of felt experiences that explore the dynamic exchanges between the personal and cultural. Together, as artists, explorers, and guides, we travel this landscape and delve into three deceptively simple, yet intertwining questions: why, how, where? "Why travel to creating dance" investigates our ontological natures: What motivates us; what is the point of the journey; and, for what purpose or goal do we travel this path? "How to travel to creating dance" is more epistemological: Is dance a habit or a vocation; what kinds of emotional, mental, and physical processes are essential to move from imagination to action; what role does uncertainty, spontaneity, and risk-taking play; what relationships, languages, vehicles do we need to reach our destinations? "Where to travel to creating dance" asks the value-laden, axiological questions: Where in the world are people creating dance and what values sustain them; what do these experiences look or feel or smell like and why (or why not) do we like them; how does creating dance come to pass, to originate and to flourish in some areas, whereas in others creating dance ceases to exist (or never exists)? Perhaps most excitingly, together these three questions address the woven tapestry of the individual, community, society, and culture that brings forth the making of meaning through infinite landscapes in dance.

We can imagine traveler's guides to creating dance in countries around the world, but we begin our journey in our homeland, the United States. We want to point out possible important landmarks and to unearth the treasure trove of back roads that may not be the most beaten paths. What road we might miss on first look and thereby lose out on a fascinating and intriguing adventure? Most importantly, the promise of our guide is the potential for further discovery. We hope that this first excursion will spark additional curiosity and study. After traveling with us, we encourage readers to journey further on their own, finding those landmarks and treasure troves that the time of an initial expedition does not permit. We hope you make many return trips.

## Traveling to Why, How, and Where

The human needs, the engagement of processes, and the values that compel us to express ourselves individually and collectively through movement have been depicted as far back as cave paintings of dancers from tens of thousands of years ago. And yet, as we all know, just because human beings are inclined—even predisposed—to dance does not suggest that the journey is a given condition. In the spirit of discovery, we offer here a traveler's guide: a collection of thoughts and experiences of those who have undertaken their own personal journeys on this road less traveled. We have asked these explorers *par excellence* to be our guides: to mark signposts, suggest interesting detours, point out places to be nourished, and provide potential itineraries based on their own personal expeditions. To gain insight into the need, motivation, and purpose for traveling to creating dance, we asked those travelers in whom we have found inspiration for our own journeys. We believe that they will inspire you too. In each of these stories, you will find a personal travelogue. In their descriptions of the connections to dance as art practice, as creative research, and as lens for understanding the world past–present–possible, we find guiding principles to answer *for ourselves* the compelling questions of "why, how, and where" to creating dance. Our hope is that this guide will assist our readers in navigating their own paths to creating dance with greater awareness of the cross-pollination of theory, practice, and culture.

## Getting Started: What to Pack

The road to creating dance necessarily entails an embodied integration of those theoretical, practical, and cultural concerns. Where the visitor may not bother to learn the history, customs, and languages of the new land, the course to creating dance embraces such a foundation. The traveler's role in creating dance is deeply personal, highly textured, and profoundly interconnected. The possibilities, questions, alternatives, and avenues produce not just something that is new, but something that is meaningful and potentially transformative. Such experiences, the unique and universal journeys alike, promise to bring forth the best in us, our art form, and in humanity. For these reasons, openness and curiosity are perhaps the most important qualities to bring on this trip.

Some food for thought in the form of big questions is good too. Travel can be arduous. Traveling to and through creating dance is a highly subjective and individual dynamic, nourished, and at times hindered, by one's societal norms. Such a trek may be filled with pitfalls and impasses, potholes and broken bridges, building one's resilience and bringing insight. To transverse such terrain can be murky, at times frightening, but potentially exhilarating. Guiding questions may help sort what William James called the "blooming, buzzing confusion" of diverse narratives. One overriding question may be about the nature and role of dance itself in human experience. What unique and common insights do these dancers share? What do these explorers tell us about what most differentiates dance and dancing from other creative arts and other skilled physical activities, such as running and sports?

For some readers, our questions may suggest a loose structure that encourages an open-ended, improvisational "backpacker" approach. Start here. Go anywhere. As in visiting any new country or in returning to a beloved well-trekked landscape, the journey can be great fun, truly exhilarating, and mind expanding in unpredictable ways that simply take off in any direction at any moment for an indeterminate amount of time. We encourage such navigation. These travelers have made their way by dancing down the path. You should too. Sling on a light pack and leave the big baggage behind. Feel free to improvise the trip, beginning and ending anywhere along the way and making the expedition your own.

## Suggested Itineraries

For other readers, the sheer amount of geographic distance, the range of topographies, and variable climates suggested by this collection of essays may be more easily traversed by consulting a map and setting an itinerary. Travel invites adventure, bringing us in contact with new people and cultures. The inscription of tradition is everywhere, even when one does not fully recognize the source or comprehend its influence. Similarly, travel with *dancers*—bodies and minds inscribed by dance experience and tradition—means journeying in the company of dance *history*. In this way, personal itineraries can be connected to larger ones, the collected itineraries of an entire discipline. Below, we offer three "possible itineraries" that connect the dancer to ensemble to history and back again.

### Itinerary 1: Body as Journal

Dance has a unique way of inscribing the body. A life in dance—as humanly organized movement with aesthetic intention—ingrains the individual with a set of dispositions. Dancers write moving identities as they dance thought through action. Such a notion stretches back in dance history at least as far as Stéphane Mallarmé, who in 1886 famously argued that the dancing body is more than a body dancing: "the ballerina is not a girl dancing . . . rather, with miraculous lunges and abbreviations, writing with her body, she suggests things which the written work could express only in several paragraphs of dialogue or descriptive prose. Her poem is written without the writer's tools" (1886/1956, p. 64).

The idea of the body as journal is unpacked in three essays that reveal the ontological nature of creativity in dance, its motivations and purposes. In Teoma Naccarato's "Recipe for a Dance Artist," we learn from this well-traveled "chef" the way a choreographer may write her moving identity through personal inspiration and creative collaboration. Her recipe-cum-methodology for making something juicy, tasty, and nourishing employs explicitly the medium of dance performance as a site for risk, rigor and relationship. "To be a dance artist, I toss in all of the vulnerability, intimacy and uncertainty I can muster and stir well, forming the batter from which nutritious and delicious dances are prepared."

John-Mario Sevilla's "To Be a Lifer: Falling to Flight" shows how the body acts as a repository of cultural and personal experiences. What's most striking about his travelogue is how he returns again and again to read and interpret the past in light of present felt experiences, revisiting his "journal" anew such that prior struggles become sources of strength and resilience. "Dance has been a quest for understanding rather than just a matter of doing, a wonderment that frequently drifts beyond knowing and before memory . . . into the one complex continuum of *becoming*, an ongoing conversation and investigation of what was, is and can be."

In Carol M. Press' "For the Love of a Question," one finds a remarkable inversion of the body as journal to journal as body. The dancing self may be understood as moving researcher, where stimulating questions derived from a curious mind animate the corporeal search for meaning. The source of creating dance is not always pre-reflective, immediate, physical experience; one also can be enthused by a reflective urge to forge new trails, to wonder aloud, to speak one's mind and body before manifesting the answer. "I discovered choreography to be an embodied quest, a dialogue between my sensory experiences that propelled movement and my intellectual endeavors that inspired reflection. Each day in the studio led to new inquiries of corporeal research . . . a circle of inquiry between the doing of choreographing, performing, reading, and writing. . . . There, if lucky, one can embrace the love of a question in all its splendor."

## Itinerary 2: Checkpoints

Anyone who has traveled extensively has encountered a checkpoint or two along the way. Checkpoints are moments of recognition: of your face and name on a passport; of your position as supplicant; of the proximity to one who holds the power of access; of the existential threat to forward progress; of your decision to take *this* route and not another. All paths, however, lead to introspection and evaluation. George Balanchine is reported to have said, "Motion in general harbors some kind of secret." How one responds to checkpoints, those moments of arrested motion, requires an inquiry into personal motivations and self-knowledge as well as the emotional and mental resources needed to arrive at one's destination. Checkpoints question what one knows and, epistemologically speaking, how one comes to understand the power of the secret in a life blessed with creating dance.

Christopher Pilafian understands these checkpoints as moments of recognition in "Stages." His early forays into the secretive world of dance eventually evolve into a life-long journey filled with choices, sudden epiphanies, and new directions. At each juncture, he shares the complicated feelings underlying the thinking dancer's decisions. His narrative of dancing in New York City in the 1970s reminds us of traveling the California coastal route on Highway 1: Each turn and bend promises an awe-inspiring vista, a new horizon to behold. But one must be wary of indulging in the view while driving this twisty route. The smart travelers keep their eyes on the road; the real route to becoming a creative artist lies in a carefully calibrated compass and keen sense of direction. Or, as Christopher says, "the work of the performing artist is the work of self-actualization." For him the secret of movement supplied his development with the "proclivities that have informed my life: introspection, curiosity, enthusiasm, and the twin thrills of falling and soaring."

If you think maps and compasses might help you navigate the maze of creating dance, then Catherine Turocy's "Spinning Spheres" is another important destination. She depicts that "vibrant tension exists between the past and the present" as she tunes into her inner compass to plot a course through, around, and sometimes over barriers that block easy access. In her struggle to forge a new path—a place for historical dance in our field—we find a powerful tale of emancipation from inner doubt and external skepticism. As Catherine reminds us, the potential for physical transformation can extend from the present not only into the future but also out of the past: "going through the actions of a written dance from almost three centuries ago sends a reverberation through my body . . . recovering the dance . . . allows the feeling of timeless existence to permeate the theater."

In "Keep Your Knees Loose & Be Ready to Jump in Any Direction," Darwin Prioleau employs the analogy of the downhill skier to suggest the twists and turns inherent in a dancing life. She faces each challenge and fork in the road with a remarkable agility, fierce intelligence, and generous sense of humor that catapults her into the upper reaches of leadership in dance. Her focus and determination reminds us not only of the fortitude that is necessary to succeed in dance, but also what the discipline of dance gives back: the confidence of our convictions and the strength of character to will our dreams into reality. As a female, African-American, and dancer, Darwin had to face many situations where her abilities were questioned, "when I had to remain strong even though I felt my confidence dwindling," but ultimately she persevered and triumphed. "I swayed on my toes just a little, gained my balance almost immediately and maintained my 'personal cool.' I knew at that moment that I could handle anything." The moral of her story is, be prepared to arrive so that, when you do, you are ready to go further than you ever imagined.

## Itinerary 3: Dance Without Borders

Look around. Does dance live in your home, office, church, or community? The ephemeral nature of dance suggests that dance exists everywhere and nowhere simultaneously; and yet, some traditions—from the sacred to the profane—have built walls around dance to circumscribe when and where dance should reside. The question of where dance begins and ends is a value-laden, axiological one that involves matters of inclusion and who gets to participate in making meaning through dance.

In "Just Do Something, Anything!" David Leventhal makes a strong case for dance without borders in the professional dance world. As a former member of the Mark Morris Dance Group, his story of personal transformation through managing and working with the Dance for Parkinson's Disease (Dance for PD) program describes how Dance for PD is part and parcel of Morris' artistic vision. As David reveals, Dance for PD is the part that extends beyond the cloistered walls of the dance company studio with unexpected results: "In the case of Dance for PD, poiesis and praxis do not merely coexist amicably side by side, separately but equally. They infiltrate and inform one another." He reminds us that dancers can and should offer more than simply our stage performances. We have a responsibility to share with others "our deep knowledge of movement and the joy we feel when we move."

Melanie Ríos Glaser knows well the power, joy, and privilege of bringing her vast knowledge to an appreciative community. As a choreographer, performer, director, and fearless wanderer, her artistic voyage wound through many ports of theatrical life. Steadfast in her bearings, she maintains, "the arts are my centering force." And yet, as she describes in "From the Floor to the Floor," her work as executive and artistic director of The Wooden Floor has been spent more on breaking down walls, broadening borders, and creating paths to participation in dance for a predominately Latino population in Southern California, than on making dances. "At The Wooden Floor, youngsters immerse themselves in dance after school hours. . . . They call The Wooden Floor their second home. . . . Here they have a space, a solid floor underneath them, and a community that supports the journey into adulthood." As a nonprofit administrator, the challenges she faces are existential and external: poverty, dropout, and desperation. As a creative artist, the challenges are more internal: The focus on others comes at the cost of personal exploration and expression. Her solution shows how one can balance the needs of creating dance for oneself and her community.

Building on the theme of moving beyond the self to the world beyond, Linda Caldwell in "Pieces of the Past Swim into the Present" makes explicit connections between her life of personal exploration to one of social action:

"I wondered, how could Nikolais' sense of moment-to-moment commitment to the performance of time, space, shape, and energy help to solve the huge social problems facing American society? Can my love of dance move beyond my own moment-to-moment enjoyment in order to spark responsible action towards the world around me? How might my personal love affair with dance become something that moves beyond my own needs?" Through a series of happy accidents and surprising twists, Linda carries these niggling questions in her proverbial backpack as she enters a doctoral program and then travels to Eastern Europe. There she records the stories of Polish dance artists that tell us as much about her own values as they do about the dance underground in Poland.

## Final Boarding Call

A wise old modern dance teacher once said that two kinds of dancers travel: tourists and explorers. Tourists desire recreation, a vacation, a glorious distraction from everyday life, an avocation to be enjoyed for its salubrious qualities. Explorers seek meaning, embarking on journeys of discovery without censorship or prearranged destination. In this view, dancer-explorers strive to learn the languages of dance; they dance as a vocation. They are drawn to the why, how, and where of creating dance as adventuresome transformation. Dancer-tourists, on the other hand, drop in and out of our world, accumulating movement vocabularies like frequent flyer miles but only skimming the surface of the culture, the art of dance. After reading this collection of essays, we can report with absolute certainty that the artists-travelers of this volume are of the explorer variety. They seek meaningful experience somewhere unvisited, for one's destination is never a place, but an embodied quest. Reading these accounts may remind you of the smart traveler's advice: If one troubles to travel, one should make the most of the luscious landscapes, secret sites, and those fellow travelers met on the way!

## Reference

Mallarmé, S. (1956). *Mallarmé: Selected prose poems, essays and letters* (B. Cook, Trans.). Baltimore: The Johns Hopkins Press. (Original work published 1886)

# 1

## For the Love of a Question

### Carol M. Press

The first day our choreography class met with Carol Scothorn, she asked if anyone wanted to show some work. A brave hand went up and my fellow graduate student ascended the small stage in the studio theater at the University of California, Los Angeles (UCLA). Before she began to dance, Carol turned to her and asked: "What do you need from us today?" Carol initiated our session with a simple question that I feel is deceptively complex. She assumed that the student showing understood her own processes and her needs at that particular creative moment in time; for us to begin to comprehend how best to watch on that particular day, and how potentially to respond most constructively, the question needed to be asked. Carol's inquiry was clearly an offer of support. Additionally, with her inclusion of "us," Carol anticipated that not only she, but also the whole class was available to investigate the dynamics of choreography and possibly assist the student further. The power of the question and the power of the group guided us through the slippery slopes of choreographing. I felt at home. Exploration was promising, even lovingly expected. The feasibility to become more, to have one question lead to another, carried me forward. Many mornings I arrived at the studios before they were opened; Carol was next to come, and with her trusty key unlocked the doors. She paved the foundation for me to draw fresh avenues on the map of my emergent quest.

My path as a dancer had been quite arduous. I knew since I was 3 years old that dance was my course, but was not allowed to study as a child. When young, my parents stopped me from doing what I loved most. Consequently, when faculty, peers, colleagues, family, and friends are supportive of my work, I let their encouragement wash through me, cleansing and refreshing. When I journeyed to college I eventually broke financial ties with my parents, put myself through school, and threw myself physically, passionately, fervently into studying dance. I was so . . . so . . . so very sore ALL the time. I ventured outside my apartment to walk half a block to the dry cleaner. I was too sore. I drove. But I was *never* too sore to dance.

I was at UCLA in graduate school working toward my choreography thesis. I do love the art form. I love moving. I am, I think, a typical dancer. In the end, I believe nothing but love could make us do what we do. Sometimes with all the pain and struggles that can be lost, but then the love comes creeping back and all is good. I was studying with fabulous teachers: choreography with Carol Scothorn (who participated in the first Judson Church performance in 1962), more choreography with Marion Scott (former member of the Martha Graham, Humphrey-Weidman, and Tamaris-Nagrin dance companies), dance ethnology with Allegra Fuller Snyder (former member of Ballet Society and Buckminster Fuller's daughter) and Elsie Dunin (Yugoslavian/Croatian researcher and dancer whose calm grace always inspired me), dance education with Melinda Williams, dance kinesiology with Martin Tracy, dance philosophy with Pia Gilbert, ballet with Mia Slavenska (former prima ballerina of the Ballet Russe de Monte Carlo), and modern dance (the foundation of my great love) with Martha Kalman (who taught me the most about my center), Chris Burnside (who always talked about his training with pioneering modern dancer Hanya Holm), Kathe Howard, and the host of guest artists from major companies who traveled through UCLA to share their talents. I was so busy that even though I ate three meals a day I kept losing weight. I am 5'2" and when I reached 101 pounds I thought enough was enough. For one week I ate four meals daily, including delicious macaroni and cheese, and my weight stabilized. I trekked to Santa Barbara almost every weekend to see my future husband Nicholas and take ballet class from the phenomenal Valerie Huston. I indeed was steeped in love.

Carol's initial question had bonded our graduate choreography class together as colleagues. We flourished creatively through the power of the question and the power of the group. A wonderful peer collective, they affectionately called me the "philosopher" because I always asked the most questions. I believed the mystery was in the details. How could I miss out on pursuing a good mystery? So I always asked questions, and pondered about what we choreographically shared and what we studied. I read and read. Connections intrigued me. Technique, supplying a physical foundation of study, philosophically fascinated me, still does. I felt that within the boundaries of embodying those special skills that allowed me potentially to execute dance fluently and eloquently laid the implementation of tools for my fulfilling life—moving from center, achieving intention and motivation, expanding beyond the perceivable. I had not noticed that I repeatedly asked questions in technique class, until one day, in response to my query Valerie exclaimed that I always had great questions and she loved that. Grateful, I continually felt at home and surrounded by exceptional people.

As I believe we all do, I carried forward into life those proficiencies praised and encouraged during my childhood. I remember that as the youngest in my family, I had the honor of answering the four questions required at our rather secular Passover Seders. The *Haggadah*, the *Book of Exodus*, contained the important responses. I gleaned from my Jewish heritage a great love of food, the wonderment of dancing at celebrations, the inspiration of a question, and the awe of knowledge encased in a book. Questions—the roads of inquiry—guided my passage. My quest for knowledge supported not just my intellectual existence, but distinctly enhanced my spiritual and daily life. Hence, I discovered early my love for excavating knowledge.

No surprise then that while at UCLA questions kept dancing around my brain. Readings and class discussions swirled around the notion that creative processes in dance were conduits for self-expression. I agreed but felt slightly uneasy. What did we mean by "self"? How can we begin to unpack that experience and discuss engagement if we have no working definitions of self? Self was elusive, something that we felt intuitively and took for granted, but I wanted more; I wanted mysterious details! Thus began a lifelong quest for mysterious details regarding creativity and self-experience. Not "self" as an objective noun, but "sense of self" as the textures and patterns that lead us through life, that constitute our being, and mark the phenomenological doing of dance. I heeded D. W. Winnicott's (1970/1986) words: "Creativity is . . . the doing that arises out of being" (p. 39). I wanted to explore my greatest love and passion experientially through the doing of dancing, questioning, reading, writing, pondering, and through the multitude of mysterious details.

I discovered choreography to be an embodied quest, a dialogue between my sensory experiences that propelled my movement and my intellectual endeavors that inspired reflection. Each day in the studio led to new inquiries of corporeal research. Why was I there at that moment in time? Why was this meaningful? How did what I created yesterday relate to what might evolve now? How did my body feel today? Where did my corporeal spontaneity pull me in relation to my past, my present, my possibilities, to the texture and patterns that constitute my sense of self and others? Where did my dancing transport my being at that particular instant through space and time and with energy?

I discovered my love of gesture, most specifically of my hands, their capacity to touch textures, elaborate patterns, and define my aesthetic presence. I realized as I spent time in the studio that my hands drew me into a wide range of sensations. I loved that sensory impressions that emerged from my hands evolved into motion through my whole body, amplifying something essential. My choreography reflected my gestural push. My written scholarship did as well as I sought to understand nonverbal aesthetic qualitative dynamics, which for me so often began in the depth of my palms.

My search invited me to cross disciplines. After finishing my master's degree in choreography at UCLA, I poured myself into the writings of Heinz Kohut, the pioneering father of psychoanalytic self psychology. Originally Freudian in outlook, he grew to believe that empathic relationships occupied the core of our psychological development, not biological drives. Thrilling to my search, Kohut asserted that a major component of a healthy sense of self was the capacity to partake in meaningful creative productivity. Studying Kohut was hard work. His thoughts persistently expanded the horizon and if one did not read all of his many volumes, one definitely missed important progressions. So with excitement for this new voyage I read everything he wrote at least twice. Perhaps influenced by his original Germanic language, Kohut wrote in long elaborate sentences masterly incorporating semi-colons. For 2 years I read nothing but Kohut; for 2 years after that my own writing had a terrible case of semi-colonitis.

My transdisciplinary questioning adventure led me to pursue a doctorate degree in interdisciplinary studies in dance and clinical psychology at Columbia Teachers College in New York City. I wanted to unite interesting links across disciplines. My dissertation looked at a cross-pollination of perspectives on choreographic process in modern dance and the writings of Kohut on creativity. Again, I worked with fabulous professors who were always available to present new questions. Penny Hanstein encouraged me to analyze through a cross-modal lens and to cultivate a sense of humor while doing so. Maxine Greene taught me the value of philosophically examining the core of aesthetic engagement. Rosalea Schonbar fortified my constant studies in psychology. I will forever be grateful that my doctoral dissertation chair, Nancy Brooks Schmitz, told me: "Don't make your dissertation your book, do your book afterward." So I did just that after looking for a whole host of new questions.

I earned my doctorate, continued to choreograph, and increased my involvement by attending professional conferences in dance organized by the Congress on Research in Dance, the Society of Dance History Scholars, the National Dance Association, and later on the National Dance Education Organization (NDEO). Such conference work augmented my journey considerably. I encountered a wide range of individuals seeking questions and investigations. I became part of a dynamic field and began to present my ideas emphasizing an integration of theory and practice in the art form. I was enriched by the work of others, pushed further, and explored more vehemently what was meaningful for me within this much broader context. Besides forming networks with colleagues, I found friends whose work widened my panoramic views of choreographing and publishing.

Additionally, I attended conferences sponsored by the International Association of Psychoanalytic Self Psychology, a field, which in line with a founder who had challenged the prevailing establishment, was itself filled with individuals finding new questions and now moving beyond Kohut. Here I could ask questions directly of authors I had read, connecting fine points on my map as I navigated new avenues of thought. I loved when a conversation moved my mind beyond where my thoughts were gently hovering. I read more and more. I began to present at these conferences as well, including performing my choreography, and to publish my scholarship on dance and creativity in psychoanalytic journals. Sustained by my love of dancing, all these pathways were traversed to expand understanding the depths of embodiment. I felt a circle of inquiry between the doing of choreographing, performing, reading, and writing, each enhancing the examination and advancement of the other.

After 5 years of research, I wrote my book *The Dancing Self: Creativity, Modern Dance, Self Psychology and Transformative Education* (2002). I incorporated the exciting expansions occurring in self psychology since Kohut's death in 1981, and brought them to bear on the relationship of dance to the individual, group, society, and culture. I concentrated on one's "sense of self," because "self" is not a thing but an experience, and drew ties to creative processes in choreographing and teaching. Most importantly, I pursued a line of questioning and thought regarding what made dance and art meaningful to ourselves and the worlds in which we live. Why bother to create? Why are we as a species compelled toward aesthetic experience? How does such mutuality among humanity enhance the profound necessity we have for diversity? Where are the landscapes that evoke us to creative engagement? Why, how, where, the cornerstones of reflective yearnings, provided perspective trails for unraveling corporeal mysteries.

Significantly, the pursuit of questions brought the fluid formation of answers. Research, whether embodied through choreographic work or written scholarship, requires the construction of choices. I experienced no profound difference between my theoretical and my physical inquiries. Even further they all felt directly related to my life. Questions, investigations, choices, created the landscape for my mind–body connections and the determinations I made living.

I used all the work I had put into my book, and into my choreography, to launch my new expeditions searching for mysterious details and adventuresome questions. With that came a yearning for collaboration; as my colleagues and I comingled our diverse and similar directions, the mysterious details expanded exponentially. Within self psychology, George Hagman was writing about creativity and aesthetics. For 10 years, we have facilitated workshops, partnered on presentations, and entered the land of co-authorship. Around the same time, I went to hear Edward Warburton speak on the importance of symbol formation as language in dance at a NDEO conference. As I sat there, I realized that all he said translated into the language of self psychology and vice versa, and with that came enrichment from weaving associations into new tapestries. Presenting, guiding workshops, and writing together my horizons have indeed stretched. Continually, my choreographic journey takes twists and turns as I collaborate with an exceptionally gifted composer, Leslie Hogan, who repeatedly creates inspiring original music. Through examining links between the questions of others and mine, I search for more exciting mysteries and quests. I take to the road anew extending my emergent map into fresh pathways. My latest love is exploring the evolving relations among contemporary neuroscience, creativity, and dance.

I still choreograph and theatrically perform. I still take dance classes, at times from the phenomenal Valerie Huston, and frequently from the exquisite Nancy Colahan. I am indeed steeped in love. I now also incorporate weight lifting and swimming into my training. I still present my scholarship and choreography conjointly; my latest such expedition was to the Spoleto Arts Festival in Italy. I still read a great deal and write and publish crossing disciplines. I additionally teach dance academics at the University of California, Santa Barbara. At times, my students will ask a question that we tackle together. Usually the discussion leads to a new question, and momentarily the students are perplexed. Did they not just successfully answer a question? Have they failed? I then reassure them that that is the exhilaration of doing research; one question ultimately leads to another as mysterious details unfold. There, if lucky, one can embrace the love of a question in all its splendor.

## Reference

Winnicott, D. W. (1986). Living creatively. In C. Winnicott, R. Shepherd, & M. Davis (Eds.), *Home is where we start from: Essays by a psychoanalyst* (pp. 39–54). New York: Norton. (Original work published 1970)

# 2

## Spinning Spheres

### Catherine Turocy

Spinning until I am dizzy and then suddenly stopping, I feel the ongoing-ness of dance and know no such thing as stillness. I am spinning, paths in space flying from an inner world and flinging outward from a central force, grounded by bent knees and dropped weight into the floor. As a child, I comfort myself by spinning and imagining a world beyond the present, a world not fixed and rigid. Children playing and fighting, parents yelling, all disappear with spinning and dancing.

Too many people are in one house, too much talking and chaos for my father. Wearing a mask behind a wall of silence, I am safe from criticism and corporal discipline. Speaking with my eyes, gestures, attitudes, I com-municate to my siblings but never "talk back" to my parents. One of many bodies, I quietly maneuver out of danger. I am already dancing, navigating a path through a difficult maze.

Five children were born within 5 years, my twin, Tom, and I the "babies" until the other three children arrived. With so much movement under one roof, our mother, at least once a day, turned on the radio declaring: "Time for us to dance!" We all pushed back the chairs and stomped, spun, tumbled, and stood on our heads as we leaned our legs against the cool green tiled wall in the kitchen. Six bodies in happy motion; this was heaven.

My eldest brother, John, had wanted to play the piano, but my father discouraged him. A musician was not a career that could provide a living for a family. My father, after returning home from a prisoner of war camp in World War II, had decided to put aside his violin and become a mail carrier for the U.S. Postal Service. But he continued to play most evenings after putting us to bed. My sister Chris, on the other hand, was allowed to study piano. She was a girl and could be a teacher. The children could only choose to study something that my parents believed could provide a means of financial independence. I was thankful that my parents thought dance fell into that category. I began instruction the following year at the age of 5. An incredible world opened beyond my life at home and now the maze became even more complex.

## Getting on the Map

My first road on the map to becoming a dancer was studying with Miss Betsy. She taught ballet, tap, hula, and acrobatics. Her large living room in a Victorian house was the local ballet studio for Solon, Ohio. Chris and I started lessons. Recitals were held in the spring on an outdoor temporary stage in her backyard. My first role was as a "Morning Glory" and, being the youngest, I was in front leading the group. Only one thing was wrong. Miss Betsy was not dancing in front of me. I had not understood that I had to memorize the dance sequence. Somehow I got through the recital, twisting my head around almost 180 degrees to watch the moves of those who knew the steps. Miss Betsy's kindness assured me this had been a miscommunication. She explained the learning process and then made me "class demonstrator" in exchange for extra lessons. I learned to memorize the steps.

As the year passed, my sister excelled at acrobatics; however, my parents decided she should focus on the piano. Today, she teaches piano for the Cleveland Institute of Music. Tom was not offered dance lessons so I taught him enough moves to be my partner for school events where we performed a *pas de deux.* But our partnership ended in second grade when he learned from the other boys in class that dancing was for "sissies." Today, Tom is in the Merchant Marines off the coast of Africa.

## Northwest to Cleveland

I am on a clear path inside the maze but now I find the trajectory must change. After 3 years, Miss Betsy announced that, for me to progress, I would need to study with a more specialized teacher. I had outgrown the world I shared with her. She arranged for me to study in downtown Cleveland with Alex Martin. He was a former dancer with the Saddler's Wells Ballet Company. He had danced in the film *The Red Shoes* (1948) and moved to Cleveland to establish a school and a company, which eventually became the Cleveland Ballet. At age 9 I was horrified when I first met him. He asked me to unlearn everything. I hit a wall in the maze that felt like a dead end. But this was Miss Betsy's idea of the next step in my career. I trusted her decision to put me in the hands of Mr. Martin. So, I backtracked, turning away from her teachings and silently trying my best to learn Mr. Martin's English ballet style. Meanwhile, I needed help with tuition. My jobs included cleaning the bathroom toilets and sinks in the studio in exchange for ballet training, which I continued to clean until I left at age 18, and teaching ballet classes for neighborhood kids in our basement and, of course, babysitting.

By the time I was 13 years old, I had become Mr. Martin's "favorite student," the one who jumped the highest, remembered all the combinations, and often was asked to participate in his lecture demonstrations. I auditioned for his company and became the youngest member. Then the Ford Foundation Scholarship Committee sent the famous ballerina, Violette Verdy, to our dance studio. As told to me by Mr. Martin, her evaluation of my dancing was that I was talented, but at 5'2" much too short for a big time ballet company like New York City Ballet. I was not offered the prestigious scholarship. With no discussion, I had hit another wall.

Alex Martin's attitude toward me changed. He wanted me to stay in Cleveland and be in his company, but I went from shining example of perfection to scapegoat when he was not in a good mood. I will not go into gruesome details. Unfortunately, he was often moody and I ended up in tears in many of his classes over the next 2 years. Holding a burning cigarette under my extended leg in second position and being forced to maintain that position for a lengthy period of time was one of his favorite tricks. But, he was still the best ballet teacher in town so I decided to "suffer for my art." The 30-minute ride home on Rapid Transit was long enough for my tears to dry and to gain my composure. I wanted no questions from my mother. I remained silent, hidden behind a mask of confusion. How could I even talk about my feelings? Doing so would only bring pain. The wall of silence was safer. No one could examine my position if I was hidden, and I would still be in control. Being told I would never be a ballerina was equivalent to being told I would never be a dancer. But in my heart I knew I was a dancer. I refused to accept one person's evaluation of my talents influenced by the Balanchine ideal body type. I had read dance history books, seen images of 18th- and 19th-century ballerinas Camargo, Sallé, Elssler, and Cerrito. I was not going to be defeated by a qualification that did not matter to me—height. I believed in a stronger intelligence in the world. I took solace in writings on choreography, poetry, and philosophy. I read the biographies of early ballerinas and the modern dance icon Isadora Duncan.

As a consolation, Mr. Martin said I could be a modern dancer—which he regarded as a lesser dance form—stay in Cleveland and dance in his ballet company. The dancers in the company were a second family to me. They were sympathetic and shared my ambitions and frustrations. They also doled out jealousy, competition, disappointment, joy, discipline, and silliness. I looked up to company member Susan McGuire who inspired me. At the time, she studied with Kathryn Karipedes at Case Western Reserve University. Overcoming challenges in her early life, she eventually became a soloist in the companies of Martha Graham and Paul Taylor, was the artistic head of the London Contemporary Dance School in England, and is currently teaching in the Dance Department at Butler University.

With Susan's encouragement, I took my first modern class. With my first exposure to the Erik Hawkins technique, I could not imagine a modern style more opposite to ballet. After 1 year of steady effort, I could articulate my spine, almost walk with a natural swing, dance in parallel position, and not always point my feet when lifted off the ground. Over time, I was exposed to other modern styles through visiting artists, master classes, and workshops in Graham and Limón. I attended a "Happening" conducted by Anna Halprin and saw a rehearsal of Alvin Ailey's company. The Joffrey Ballet came to town with contemporary ballets. However, Daniel Nagrin's *The Peloponnesian War* (1968) affected me the most. His choreography brought ancient history, the world wars, and the Vietnam War into perspective through an astonishing and charismatic performance. His use of heavy face paint showed how a mask could be used for expressing emotion instead of repressing feeling. Dance mixed with text, history, and music. The boundaries of choreography had been ripped open. I wanted to be like Nagrin, a dancer-choreographer with the power of storytelling. Finally, I was making progress in the maze. I began to sense an inner compass.

## Changing Direction

To dance was to improvise. To choreograph was to record improvised phrases and to arrange them for my fellow students at St. Jude's School and later Orange High School. I always chose the dance phrase for a reason and I worked to convey that reason to my friends. With Mr. Martin, choreography was different. Once I asked him in rehearsal what the dance phrase meant. I wanted to know how best to perform the movement. "Be quiet and dance," was his answer. So I was, and I did, until I was 18. Always, I found staying behind a wall of silence was safer. I was not attacked for my thoughts or feelings when behind the wall. But not knowing what the dance phrases meant when performing choreography, other than my own, made me a cautious and hesitant performer. I executed the steps but never felt as if I danced inside the music. I often was behind the beat. In retrospect, I imagine Mr. Martin had some source of inspiration, but he did not infuse his dancers with these ideas and degraded us for asking questions. When I graduated from high school I wrote him a letter about our love-hate relationship, having just discovered this concept in English literature by reading Graham Greene. I have no idea what he did with the letter. More importantly, this letter served as my declaration of independence and the first crack in the wall of silence. I finally said what was on my mind and I anxiously waited for some sort of reply. None came, but at least nothing bad happened. I never had to see him again and I never did.

## Searching for the Next Road

My parents clearly stated that I would be on my own after graduating from high school. My options were few: pay my own way through college or go to New York City and begin auditioning for a company while working at any job I could find. Too many girls from Mr. Martin's company went to New York after graduation and came back discouraged, dropping out of dance completely. New York was the largest city in North America. How could I hope to handle the transition on my own without more preparation? By now I had already been employed as a professional choreographer for two summer musicals while still in high school. I wanted to choreograph and have my own company. After much reflection, soul searching, and reading, I decided to go to college. I hoped to gain more understanding of the performing arts, literature, philosophy and anything else that would prepare me in my chosen field. The Ohio State University (OSU) offered financial aid and a work/study program to help with expenses. Now, in the larger arena of more than 50,000 students, the very nature of the maze changed. I began to trust my inner compass to help maneuver around the blind spots.

OSU was a top choice for a modern dancer. Classes included ballet, improvisation with Lynn Dally, and modern dance composition with Ruth Currier and later, Peter Saul. Labanotation was with Lucy Venable, and former dancers in the Humphrey/Limón, Taylor and Cunningham companies taught modern technique classes. I was thrilled to take the required classes of costume and lighting design, and publicity, which taught us how to write press releases. Folk, ballroom, and African dance plus a course in fencing were available to us and, of course, dance history. My life was 7 to 11. Beginning the day with working in the cafeteria at 7 a.m., I went to my academic and dance classes and then rehearsed in the studio until 11 p.m. Homework was what I did in between everything else.

As a student, I joined both the modern dance company directed by Vickie Blaine and the Baroque Dance Ensemble (BDE) directed by Shirley

Wynne. The BDE evolved because Shirley and the student dancers, including me, saw an exciting future for historical dance and we wanted to be a
part of that future beyond college. We loved the music, the costumes, and
the drama. I was ecstatic! What a luxury to enjoy the beauty and passion of
the well-ordered Baroque world as well as the heady debates and chaos of
modern dance. Paradoxically, Baroque dance was so old that the form was
viewed as radical. In fact, the musicians who performed new music were the
same ones in the early music concerts springing up on campuses all over
the country. Nothing was stable and everything was questioned.

I graduated two quarters early to save money. Before leaving OSU,
however, I needed an answer to a question burning inside of me. But I was
nervous and reaching beyond the wall of silence was difficult. If I hid and
was quiet, all dreams were still possible without pain. But how was I to make
progress through this increasingly complex maze without clear direction, a
reality check? I gathered my strength and talked to the director of the OSU
dance company, Vickie Blaine. Temporarily overcoming my shyness, I asked
her if she thought I was good enough to become a dancer in New York. I knew
the answer in my heart, but I wanted to be reasonable and practical and not
blinded by my own opinion of my abilities. She said yes. What a relief for me!

## Going West

After graduation I stayed with the BDE, which had extracted itself from OSU
and journeyed to California because Shirley had taken a new post at the
University of California, Santa Cruz. The personal computer had not been
invented yet. The area was not cultured or wealthy enough to support six
professional Baroque dancers. Plans for the company gradually came undone.
I taught at the YMCA and performed my own modern works while dancing
with the BDE until the company dissolved in 1975-1976. I hit another dead
end. Some of the members had already moved to New York. I had fallen in
love with a harpsichordist in New York and was carrying on a long-distance
relationship. Clearly, my compass pointed east.

## Going East

In January 1976, I relocated to New York; moved in with my boyfriend,
James Richman; was disowned by my parents; produced a concert of my
modern dance works; and founded The New York Baroque Dance Company
with my close friend, Ann Jacoby. Because opera-ballet requires more than
two dancers, and we wanted to raise funds to pay the dancers and protect
them with workman's disability insurance, we incorporated as a nonprofit,

starting the process in August 1976. Our first self-produced concert was with Concert Royal, directed by my harpsichordist boyfriend Jim. Performing with musicians with whom we worked so closely, examining every detail was incredible. Additionally, I was thrilled to finally work with more dancers and to play with complicated choreographic designs. We received a decent review from music critic John Rockwell, who failed to see we wore masks and wondered why our faces did not change expression.

Before I go on with my journey, and for those who are keeping track of my other jobs, please add amusement park ride operator, children's clothes store clerk, dance notation tutor, periodical librarian assistant, costume seamstress, human resource head hunter assistant, and summer camp counsellor/dance teacher at Camp Starlight. In 1977, Jim and I married and my family took me back into the fold.

## Using My Inner Compass

By 1979, money and time were being stretched to their limit. As a choreographer I had been self-producing and promoting my modern and historical creations. I knew a choice had to be made. I needed to focus my resources in one direction before I ran into another wall. I will forever be grateful to my dear friend, Joshua Karter, a theater director and teacher. His question was simple: "Did dance need another modern choreographer or a professional who dedicated her career to the new field of historical dance performance?" He asked me to consider not what I wanted to do, but what was best for the dance field. What was needed by this art form? How did my own talents fit with the larger picture? In my mind, I could hear the strains of an earlier call to action: "Ask not what your country can do for you, ask what you can do for your country" (John F. Kennedy, 1961). This conversation, this motivating idea has steadily guided my inner compass throughout my career. I needed to put my ego aside. Perhaps I find the word "compass" in compassion? Through compassion for the ongoing struggle of dance in our world today, I find a direction. If the field is not flourishing, how can I expect to flourish? Most importantly, I acknowledge Jim, my boyfriend and later husband and father of my children, whose constant love, irritation, and understanding has sustained me through my journey.

## My Compass Leads to New York City

While New York in the 1970s was a "Golden Age" for dance, and continues to be a magnet for aspiring artists, I believe my explorations into period dance were just as valid as experiments of choreographers with the Judson Dance

Theater. We all used a dance vocabulary closer to everyday movement than the more virtuosic style of classical ballet. Many of us experimented with expression in geometrical paths through space. The most striking difference, which set me apart in both the worlds of modern and period dance, was my exploration into the Baroque use of the mask. No "how-to" books were written on the subject. The mask was part of the uniform of the Baroque dancer in the 17th and 18th centuries; yet none of my colleagues used the mask in their reconstructions. They saw the mask as just a costume item. Soon, by wearing the mask in all my performances, I ventured deeper into the journey of the soul. I sought "the knowledge of the mask," as discussed in 18th-century writings. In wearing a mask one cannot speak. However, in the 20th century, wearing the mask was radical. I was constantly asked to talk about the mask and to defend my decisions in reconstructing Baroque dances. My ideas were attacked and, as I had learned before, I could not hide behind a wall of silence.

## Knowledge of the Mask Rises

I needed to find my voice. Jim helped me to understand that silence was no longer an option. Through his love, persistent questioning, and insistence that I not walk away, I sorted out my own emotions and feelings. Finding clarity in my personal life allowed for more growth. My early Catholic education taught me that anger and even just thinking a bad thought were venial sins. Years of repressed feelings clouded decisions and actions. None of this mattered to Jim. We had long conversations about religion, the sexual revolution, art, the history of science, and so forth. My relationship with him began to affect the way I interacted with others. I became more articulate and confident. For example, I read a review of our concert that I thought was unjust and I wrote to the critic. He saw my point and we began a constructive dialogue. In another case, musicologists and scholars attacked my interpretation of 18th-century dance notation as being "too expressive." I was stunned, but recovered quickly. I began more in-depth research in order to build a solid argument with facts and statements to support intuitive decisions of interpreting printed documents, dance treatises, and notations. By finding a voice to defend my artistic decisions, I soon realized that I had, in fact, followed an inner compass on my journey through life. I began to trust my feelings and instincts with more confidence.

After finding my own voice, I became a voice for the dancers of past centuries. In the 1970s recreating dances from 18th-century notation was still a field for pioneers. Few professional dancers were involved in period dance performances. One was more likely to find professors, students, and musicologists who had never taken a dance class recreating minuets and chaconnes. Poor decisions on the execution of a step were the result of an untrained body joined with an untrained mind, one that lacked experience as choreographer, director or dancer. I was disturbed at what I witnessed in the field. Trusting my instincts and stage experience, I focused on bringing alive the pages of dance notation from 250 years ago. I took educated guesses on the answers to questions of interpretation not fully documented. I created theories and offered convincing proofs of how gestures from the art of declamation found in 17th- and 18th-century treatises may have been used in theatrical dance. My publications were not books, but performances. Program notes for our concerts were so extensive they were cited in academic papers. According to the magazine, *Ballet News*, I became a "Baroque dance activist." In 1979, I was one of the founding members of the Society of Dance History Scholars. I also gave lectures and master classes on the subject of period dance reconstruction. My passion for the subject helped me get pass my shy nature. I taught more and, through teaching and directing the dancers in my company, I became a better performer, stage director, and choreographer. I was no longer in a maze but an evolving sphere, revolving all around the discovery of the mask.

## The Mask Illuminates the Way

My secret was to find the "knowledge of the mask," to uncover truth and beauty in gesture. In wearing the mask, I become aware that the audience does not see me, Catherine Turocy. I put that person aside when I don the mask and the costume. I become both the puppet and the puppeteer. I feel every nerve in my body. I experience a complete state of joined body and mind in the physical world, and at the same time, I experience a disembodied self who directs the movements from above and behind my body. I achieve what Diderot (1830) described in his acting treatise, *Paradoxe sur le Comédien*, beginning to understand what he meant by "representation."

How strange to feel as if I have been liberated from the physical world simply by wearing a mask. The audience becomes kinesthetically involved. They use their animal instincts to watch the dancer because they cannot see the face, the usual source of communication. Every gesture is magnified and has meaning. Any forgotten limb or misplaced breath detracts from the performance. Every performance with the mask is part of the journey going deeper into the "knowledge of the mask." The process can only take place on stage and is practiced by performing. Now the stage becomes a "sacred ground" where only truth exists and the dance is a communal experience, taking performer and audience to a pre-language existence, one without words. This is where I dwell. This is the exploration into early dance that keeps me sustained and motivates my actions. I reach a sense of multidimensional time.

Even today, going through the actions of a written dance from almost three centuries ago sends a reverberation through my body. The hours spent recovering the dance are now reduced and refined to passing moments as the music carries my body across the stage. The mask allows the feeling of timeless existence to permeate the theater. Representation through the costume, the mask, the gesture, the artifice of the dance, allows for a shared experience so difficult to describe in words. Perhaps the art itself is complete, and is not about words? Dance is time and space and in historical dance the audience experiences layers of culture still vibrating, breathing in the life of today. This deeper experience of history hints at the future to come. If we can dance to the right, we can dance to the left; if we can dance backward, we can dance forward, all in time and space.

## New Passages

Up to now I have written about my experiences through a dancer's eyes. But what happens as I age and my body is no longer the perfect instrument? For me, this is the most difficult passage. My hips are not as flexible and I find turning out difficult. My jump is closer to the ground and my balance is not as steady. I am thankful for the mask and wig which help to disguise the outer appearances of age. Historical dance technique is related to natural movement and allows one to perform well into one's 40s and 50s. Comic and character dances are possible to perform to one's last breath. But this is an exception to most dancers' stories.

How beautiful for our world if dancers recognized the importance of being a Muse of the Dance. The Muses are the Daughters of Memory who keep the arts and sciences alive in spite of war and natural destruction. They preserve the flame of knowledge and inspiration for future generations. How different our society would be today if more active dancers recognized they were muses and could find their own way to keep the flame burning after leaving the stage. Retired performing dancers could better serve so many areas of dance. Why wait for retirement before exploring areas of dance that are not on the stage?

Dance writing, criticism, research, history, theory, and analysis are all valuable during any period of one's dance career. At any age, one can teach dance for health and recreational purposes that not only builds an audience for dance, but also more importantly, allows the general public to enjoy health benefits of the mind–body experience of dance in a communal setting. Our field suffers a brain drain because dancers are not made aware of these opportunities earlier in their training. When they retire, many go into completely different fields and some suffer from a long and lingering depression.

In my own story, I perform less. I teach, direct operas, choreograph, and mentor dancers more. Growing up in a large family (and having my own sons Andrew and Edward with Jim) gave me a keen sense of community and responsibility to others. Having a company has been a blessing. Now my dream is to establish the Early Dance Institute in a major dance department that will work along with our company. We need a laboratory of research to keep our work fresh and expanding. I want to create a sphere where young dancers of the institute train in historical dance and perform along with the more experienced dancers of The New York Baroque Dance Company. In turn, our company dancers can teach at the institute, coach young performers and choreographers in reconstruction and be consultants to scholars. I want the institute to develop scholars who cross disciplines and join the history of dance with the other arts and sciences at a very deep level. The field is ready to expand. I also hope through a university to establish educational programs for children K-12, integrating dance into the teaching of history, geometry and physical education.

## Still Spinning

For me, a vibrant tension exists between the past and the present. Eternal symbols, metaphors and gestures are embedded in dance formulas, manifested through plastic poses, rhythm, and geometrical patterns through space. Everything exists in relation to an opposite. North and South, East and West, I must be ready to embrace the full range of extremes and everything in between them. Through my inner compass I see and select directions. I do not have control over what happens to me in life, but I do have the power to choose how I react. My walls have fallen. I have come out my maze. My mask guides me. Connecting between my inner universe and the Dance of the Spheres, I still spin.

## Reference

Diderot, D. (1830). *Paradoxe sur le comédien*. Paris: A. Sautelet and Company.

3
———

# Stages

Christopher Pilafian

## Spiral and Fall

On the first Wednesday of eighth grade, I was introduced to modern dance. Our teacher, Norma Carter, challenged us to create a short study incorporating techniques and ideas we had studied during the class. Gathering my body into a low crouch to start, I uncurled as I rose along a tight spiral path, accelerated to an explosive jump with a reach to the sky, and plunged to earth in a sideways fall. Looking back, I see in this little dance my boyish excitement about starting a new adventure, my aspiration to challenge limits, my taste for speed and the thrill of surrendering to momentum. Within that 7-second kinetic study lie clues to proclivities that have informed my life: introspection, curiosity, enthusiasm, and the twin thrills of falling and soaring.

## Norma Is Going to Love You

Two days earlier, I transferred from the Detroit public school I had attended since kindergarten—an educational environment that seemed to become more chaotic every day—to the small, serene Roeper School, 90 minutes outside the city. At the end of my first day, while waiting for the bus home, I lounged with a group of classmates on a grassy slope outside the school. One of my classmates said something that prompted me to share a yoga relaxation exercise I had learned from my mother. These new friends listened willingly and offered me a sweet first teaching experience. A comment afterward, "You have to meet Norma; she is going to love you," aroused my curiosity.

Norma Carter studied with Hanya Holm, who was one of the leading pioneers of modern dance. Norma came close to "going professional" as she used to say, then circumstances brought her to Roeper where she taught and inspired generations of students until her retirement. Norma offered a stimulating mix of technique and creative play in her classes. We regularly incorporated her lessons about time, space, and energy into our improvisations and compositions. She taught us to revel in the propulsive intensity or delicate beauty of Vivaldi, Beethoven, and other great composers as well as contemporary artists like the Beatles and jazz harpist Dorothy Ashby. She had an orange-and-white parachute and two enormous pieces of billowing blue and violet silk. We played ecstatically with these, learning about weightlessness, suspension, flow, and group cooperation. She also taught us exercises that she had learned directly from Joseph Pilates, renowned inventor of the eponymous core-fitness method.

## Embodying Actuality

I had performed on stage at the age of 3 and worked as a professional child actor since the age of 9 but that December I experienced my first dance performance, a structured improvisational piece to Benjamin Britten's *Ceremony of Carols*. The music created an atmosphere like freshly fallen snow in moonlight. At one point in the dance, while spiraling counterclockwise to a half-kneel to face another dancer, I realized that, unlike my earlier performing experiences, I was neither pretending nor *representing* anything. The mystical spell of the music combined with the sensation of moving purposefully and collaboratively through space and time gave rise to a new awareness of being. I experienced embodied actuality. A wave of kinesthetic awareness poured through me like light through an open window.

Later that year, I attended a performance in the elegant Kresge Court of the Detroit Institute of Art featuring a group of women dancing in Renaissance costumes. The choreography, I later learned, was derived from the treatise *Orchésographie* originally published in 1589 by Thoinot Arbeau, a French dancing master. I was already interested in Renaissance and Baroque art and architecture and felt attracted to the period movements and costumes. I was not as happy about seeing the men's roles played by women in what I saw as "Doris Day pageboy drag."

Harriet Berg was and is the artistic director of the Festival Dancers. I met her immediately after the show and offered my unvarnished 14-year-old opinion. To my surprise, she invited me to join the troupe. A formative apprenticeship followed, during which I studied and performed a repertoire of 16th-century dances. As the only teenager in the group, I learned from the examples of the adults. Outside of classes and rehearsals, Harriet frequently made me aware of aspects of life and art I had not yet experienced such as the works of Louise Nevelson, Henry Moore, Martha Graham and Marcel Proust. When I read Ayn Rand, she cautioned me by saying, "Careful; that's only half the picture." Harriet's mentorship was the force that launched me onto a career path in dance.

## In Grief, an Opening

My mother was diagnosed with cancer when I was 14 years old. She died two years later. The youngest of four children, I lived with my father, Suren Pilafian. An architect by profession and a cellist by avocation, he was a very internal person, intensely thoughtful with a sense of humor. In the performing arts he preferred participation to spectatorship. A few weeks after my mother's death, for reasons he did not explain, he enrolled in a chamber music retreat at Interlochen Music Camp in northern Michigan and invited me to come along. I believe he chose the retreat as a balm for our loss.

Five hours north of Detroit, in the little finger of Michigan's mitten shape, my father played chamber music while I explored the grounds of Interlochen. I strolled among dozens of freestanding practice cabins scattered throughout the woods, sketchpad in hand, pausing to listen as a Schubert piano trio, a Brahms string quartet, reedy woodwinds, or tootleing recorders—the sounds of musicians coming together to do what they loved—merged with the natural environment. Witnessing nature and listening to music seemed to deepen the dream-like state in which I had been living since my mother's death.

In a clearing beyond the cabins, I came upon a newer building. The doors were open so I went inside to explore. I found a long concourse with displays regarding the recently inaugurated Interlochen Arts Academy (IAA), a winter counterpart to the summer camp. Here were samples of student writings, artworks on paper and canvas, photos of orchestras, bands, singers, actors, and dancers. I was fascinated by images of dancers my age, including boys looking trained and confident and girls *en pointe*. Having discovered this place, I returned repeatedly during the week, wanting to step into the world these images represented.

I had heard about Juilliard and I understood that attending Interlochen, a nationally recognized, pre-professional arts high school, would help me move in that direction. In the fall, I met with George Roeper, the headmaster of Roeper School and laid out my plan. He was supportive, so I started the process of transferring to IAA for senior year. Because both parents were architects, I had been educated about drawing, painting, and color theory, in addition to my early training in acting, so I applied to the visual art, drama, and dance programs.

## A Brush with Greatness: The Limón Company in Detroit

Two years earlier when I was 14, the José Limón Dance Company visited Detroit for a 1-week residency funded by the Dance Touring Program of the National Endowment for the Arts (NEA). The Dance Touring Program was credited with tripling the national audience for dance performance in just 3 years. During their residency, the Limón Company conducted daily master classes and lecture demonstrations throughout the greater Detroit area. Both Norma Carter and Harriet Berg made sure their students attended as many of these as possible. Norma bundled her four most avid aspirants (including me) into her car to drive us long distances for these opportunities. Harriet hosted a series of Limón master classes at the Jewish Community Center (where for 3 years I took weekly classes and rehearsed with her teen group, The Young Dancers' Guild).

In this way, I was introduced to Limón's vocabulary based on the *fall and rebound* principle. I have many vivid memories of this week. For example, while learning material from José's *There is a Time* (1956), Daniel Lewis instructed us to *drop* our head sideways. This action triggered an "Aha!" moment. I heard my body say, "Of course—this makes perfect sense!" I recognized the very same surrendering to gravity that had made an impression on me in my first modern dance class with Norma.

The IAA dance audition consisted of a technique class taught by guest artist Richard Gain, a member of the Martha Graham Dance Company. The class was more technically exacting than anything I had studied and, although I gamely followed along, the Graham technique does not yield to mere imitators. I was not accepted as a dance major but was offered a scholarship from the drama department. I remained undeterred, however, in my intention to dance, confident that I would find a way. That summer, I received a letter from Interlochen announcing a complete turnover of the  dance faculty. I read the enclosed professional biography of the new modern dance teacher, Nona Schurman, and felt a rush of relief and excitement when I saw that she had danced with the Humphrey-Weidman Dance Company. I knew that José Limón's mentor had been Doris Humphrey, and that her kinetic philosophy was referred to as *fall and recovery*. Nona

Schurman was part of a lineage with which I identified. I felt the door of possibility opening wider.

## Enter Avatars

Toward the end of the Limón residency in Detroit, Jennifer Muller and Louis Falco arrived. Their delayed appearance seemed to confer on them a kind of celebrity status, reinforced by the excited anticipation expressed by dancers more experienced than I. The residency included a 2-day mini-intensive at a seminary some distance from Detroit that I attended under Harriet's mentorship. Jennifer and Louis taught separate and simultaneous classes the first day. Due to the high regard in which Harriet held Louis, he had acquired mythic proportions in my imagination. All my dance teachers up to that time had been women and I was excited to have an opportunity to learn from a male dancer. So, without question, I signed up to take Louis's class.

With his movie star good looks and golden corona of hair, Louis was the most charismatic man I had ever seen. Just being in the same room with him was a memorable experience. Taking his class was electrifying. While we were at *barre* in a *degagé* position—an unaccustomed place for me—he took my right calf in his hands and directed me to relax my leg. I heard the words but they were incomprehensible because *he was touching my leg.* He then looked up at me from his crouch and asked, "Is your leg relaxed?" Frozen and mute, I managed a nod, hoping I was being truthful, although, honestly, I could not feel my leg at all, so riveted was I by the proximity, attention, and physical contact of this Apollo-in-the-flesh. His vibrancy, sanguinity, self-confidence, and technical command seemed otherworldly. After another second or two, he gave a rueful shrug and let go of my leg, leaving me to sort out what had just happened.

After *barre*, Louis taught us part of "Pegasus," a solo from Limón's *The Winged* (1966). At one point he demonstrated a *promenade,* a slow turn, with his right knee hooked over his right elbow at shoulder height and his shin and foot pointed out horizontally like a periscope scanning the horizon. We followed along, imitating him. As he turned, a young dancer stood at such close range that her neck was directly in the path of his shin. I figured one of two things would happen: he would pause and lower his leg to avoid hitting her or she would step away to give him space. Neither occurred. Louis calmly raised his shin and foot until they pointed directly to the ceiling, cleared the young dancer's head and calmly returned his leg to its prior position. As far as I knew, male dancers were not expected to do such things. A soft gasp went through the room. Louis had challenged our preconceptions.

## The Buzz

After class, as I digested the "Falco effect," I heard the excited buzz in the hallway among those who had taken Jennifer Muller's class. They reported how illuminating she was, how compellingly she communicated ideas with wonderful, cogent imagery, inspiring demonstration and beautifully structured phrases. I remember wishing I could have taken both classes.

The Limón residency culminated in a performance by the entire company in the Ford Auditorium in downtown Detroit. The program included *The Moor's Pavane* (1949), danced by Clyde Morgan as Othello, Betty Jones as Desdemona, Louis Falco as Iago, and Jennifer Muller as Amelia. All four were first-rate performers. At intermission, however, I noticed again that the buzz was about Jennifer: the arc, sweep, and power of her performance. After listening to these comments, I replayed the piece in my mind. I saw Jennifer's lush, full movement, propelled by something I did not comprehend. I was able to perceive a kind of freedom and volume in her use of weight and line. I discerned a difference between hers and Betty's modulated, beautiful, but seemingly more demure presence. Whereas Betty remained a highly regarded artist, Jennifer generated excitement.

## Paradigm Shift

In 1970, Harriet arranged for me to attend the American Dance Festival (ADF). A school friend invited me to fly in his family's small plane, piloted by his dad. With the excitement of a great adventure, that flight catapulted me into a new chapter of life as the tiny plane buzzed between clouds, over farms, towns, mountains, and lakes, toward New London, Connecticut.

At ADF, I met and interacted with a spectrum of artists and methods from the New York-centric field of professional contemporary dance. I saw masters, loyalists, rebels, and renegades all engaged in a lively interplay. Personalities, egos, and esthetics competed and cross-fertilized. For decades, Martha Graham and José Limón had maintained a continuous and influential presence at the festival. Harriet told me that resistance to the status quo had resulted in neither of these great figures of modern dance attending in 1969. Yvonne Rainer stepped into the ADF limelight that year with her *Trio A* and interest rose in what was to become known as postmodernism. Between 1970 and 1972, Martha's and José's companies appeared only briefly at the festival. During these 3 years I completed high school, began my studies at Juilliard, and attended ADF three times.

## Yvonne, Erin, Rudy, Barbara, Bill, and Meredith

I witnessed and participated in numerous pedestrian-based and experimental works that eschewed or subverted conventional dance skills. These projects reflected Yvonne Rainer's 1964 NO Manifesto exhorting dancers and choreographers to reject established values:

> NO to spectacle no to virtuosity no to transformations and magic and make-believe no to the glamour and transcendency of the star image no to the heroic no to the anti-heroic no to trash imagery no to involvement of performer or spectator no to style no to camp no to seduction of spectator by the wiles of the performer no to eccentricity no to moving or being moved. (p. 178)

Along these lines, I studied Rudy Perez's Zen-like minimalism as he laid gaffers tape on the stage floor with an expert's focused intent. I watched Bill Dunas's sparse, introspective solo with bowl of water and chair in a dark, cold, downtown loft. I watched Barbara Roan's *Parade* (1971) at the Cubiculo Theater on 14th Street, in which my roommate Nancy Scher was one of two-dozen diverse characters performing idiosyncratic actions in a slow, serpentine procession. She carried a big metal saucer-shaped Coke sign, laid the sign down every 10 steps or so and struck a "ballerina" pose on top. The sign produced a loud "pop" as she stepped up and another as she dismounted. I transformed myself into one of a cluster of statues for Erin Martin's site-specific choreography in a seaside rose garden in New London. These and other "postmodern" works that I saw or performed shaped my perception of what was developing in dance at that time.

At ADF I was particularly inspired by the imagination and scale of Meredith Monk's *Needle Brain Lloyd and the Systems Kid* (1970). This 4-hour "live movie" featured horses, motorcycles, people spilling out of buildings, dropping out of trees, rowing across a lake, oozing across the grass, and dressed as pioneers migrating across a large field in painstakingly slow motion.

## When Is Less *Not* More?

The post-war mantra "less is more," associated with Mies van der Rohe, exhorts us to eliminate nonessentials. With this, and the NO Manifesto, in the air, I saw many young choreographers stripping away familiar options associated with the old guard, primarily "movement for movement's sake." The influence of John Cage and Merce Cunningham was widely evident as dancers sought liberation from clichés and time-worn choreographic methods. "Naturalness," which played a prominent role in the changing zeitgeist of the 1960s, manifested choreographically as ordinary, everyday idioms of behavior, posture and gesture, frequently performed with a flat affect.

In this context, I began to wonder if technical skill had become outmoded. Perhaps, I thought, the fact that technical proficiency is difficult to attain had some influence on emerging postmodernists' rejection of virtuosity and kinetics. I sympathized with the quest for an alternative to the status quo; however, except for Meredith's spectacular *Needlebrain Lloyd and the Systems Kid*, none of the works of the time elicited in me a desire to participate.

After moving to New York City, I attended as many dance performances as possible, especially the "cool" ones presented in downtown lofts, where the ticket price fit a student's budget. After a couple of years, the prevailing minimization of movement in the performative vocabulary and the emphasis on repetition and the "ordinary" in choreography began to wear thin for me and lose meaning, like a word repeated over and over. I noticed that my most frequent post-performance response was "Why?"


## In Contrast

Other contemporary dance artists, such as Louis Falco, Twyla Tharp, Lar Lubovitch, and Jennifer Muller were challenging the status quo in their own ways. The dancers in Louis Falco's company presented themselves on stage as everyday human beings rather than formal, stylized, or heroic personas. In this aspect, they overlapped esthetically and ideologically with emerging postmodernists. For the Falco dancers, however, being at ease in their skins (and with each other) infused their performances not only with what could be called natural, everyday behavior but also with remarkable kinetic power, freedom, and resilience. The amplitude and flair they brought to dance both beguiled and rankled critics and seemed to defy the precepts of the NO Manifesto. Within Louis's highly identifiable vocabulary and style, at once close to and far from Limón's, each dancer had a unique performing signature. They were exciting, provocative, highly individualized dancers, each so closely fused to the choreography that I had difficulty imagining anyone else performing their roles. (I expect this was true in the first generation of the Limón Company with Pauline Koner's temperament and kinetic impulse distinct from Betty Jones's and José's from Lucas Hoving's.)

## Witness the Witness

I believe that one of our greatest challenges as human beings is to imagine phenomena we have not yet seen or experienced. Witnessing a new phenomenon can redefine one's sense of possibility. For instance, at ADF I enrolled for two summers in a technique class taught by Clay Taliaferro, a tall, imposing, and charismatic man who had worked with Donald McKayle and later went on to dance many of José's parts in the Limón company. During the Falco Company's brief stint at ADF in 1972 (my third summer there), Jennifer Muller attended one of Clay's classes. After executing a phrase that traveled the length of the studio, I turned to watch Jennifer dance the same phrase. Every move she made was more fully actualized than I had imagined possible. The shapes her body made were fuller, more lived-in, her trajectories grander, impulses deeper. Her swing, curve, and twist all went further, infused with appetite for movement and with impeccable clarity. Watching her, my perception of what is possible in dance was altered, expanded, and redefined.

Thirty years later, Clay Taliaferro visited the University of California, Santa Barbara where I am on faculty. Within a few seconds after our "hellos" I brought up that incident, which I recognized as a turning point for me. Clay surprised me by saying that he too remembered and that he had been watching me as I watched Jennifer. I was unexpectedly moved by this. I had intended to thank Clay for the gift of that moment and he immediately gave me another gift—the knowledge that as my teacher he had cared enough to witness and recognize a pivotal moment in my life.

## Louis and Jennifer

Louis and Jennifer together made a charismatic duo onstage. Both passionate and powerful, they appeared to challenge each other to go beyond any limits. Every impulse one of them generated the other transmuted into something more. In relation to one another, Louis was Apollo to Jennifer's Athena. Their partnership produced an effect greater than the sum of its parts.

I recall vividly a performance at Lincoln Center's Alice Tully Hall in which Jennifer was seated on the floor in fourth position, while Louis stood behind her. They were connected somehow. From the front row I saw an impulse pass between them and travel through Jennifer's spine like a wave. She rose a few inches off the floor like silk blown by a wind, her torso, neck, and head tossing backward. She was weightless for a moment. Then she landed in an undulating forward dive. She rose and returned to earth again and again in rapid, fluid figure eights that were unlike anything I had seen. She seemed to become an aquatic creature in a roiling ocean, a dynamic, elemental embodiment of will and surrender. As she and Louis traveled together across the stage, I noticed that neither seemed to be *doing* anything, yet I saw in that brief sequence an astonishing synthesis of kinetic energy, choreographic originality, and mythic evocation. I experienced what Joseph Campbell refers to as "esthetic arrest." My mind was still. Then the thought arose: "How can they seem to be doing so little while doing so much?"

## Treeing

In June 1973, following a Falco Company season, I traveled to Detroit to visit my father. On a bright summer afternoon, while musing on the seeming universality of movement, I watched a poplar tree in full leaf bend and sway in the wind, leaves twisting and fluttering, branches tossing to and fro, many individual parts moving dynamically in countless directions. I recognized that the tree, even in that highly active state, was simply *being* a tree. The tree was, in a word, *treeing*. I saw in this phenomenon a parallel to Jennifer's dancing: In motion, she was as connected to her essential nature as this tree was to its own. When she danced, *doing* and *being* merged. I wanted to know how such a thing was possible.

## More-ness

That fall, hundreds of dancers descended on the Alvin Ailey/Pearl Lang studios on East 59th Street to audition for Louis's company. Still a student at Juilliard, but intensely curious, I slipped in with a friend to observe. At one point, Jennifer stood up from behind the table to give notes after one of the company members had taught a phrase from her choreography. Wearing street clothes and 6-inch platform shoes, she indicated parts of the phrase as she spoke. The way she moved differed from what had been demonstrated earlier. Whispering, I asked my friend what she thought made the difference. She said, "There's just so much *more movement* when Jennifer does it." Even balancing on outrageous shoes and without a warm-up, she had more quality, fullness, flow, clarity, and personal presence than anyone else in the room. Jennifer embodied the extraordinary.

## Stand and Shout

Nine months later, in June 1974, again at Alice Tully Hall, I witnessed the premiere of Jennifer's work, *Speeds*, performed by the Falco Company. I had seen her earlier ballets along with Louis's in 1972 and 1973 but my response to this particular work came as a surprise; I stood up and shouted. I quickly bought a ticket for the following night and at the end I found myself once again on my feet shouting. I felt sure I had witnessed a breakthrough in the field of contemporary dance, caught a glimpse of a larger story. I felt an affinity with the work, as if she had affirmed and reflected some inner aspiration I held. I had seen once again the poplar tree—many parts moving separately while connected.

During the curtain call, I felt strangely surprised when only seven dancers appeared. I laughed at myself when I realized that the many quick changes and mercurial performances in *Speeds* had created the illusion of a much larger cast. (Years later, as Jennifer's own company grew in numbers, the cast of *Speeds* gradually increased to 12, the version performed by the Alvin Ailey American Dance Theater. The structural integrity of *Speeds* is strong enough to sustain such expansion, but the original version defied perception by making 7 dancers *seem* like 12.)

## An Offering

A week or so later, I called Jennifer and requested to meet her. As an offering, I carefully chose some large, deep purple plums with bloom still frosting the skin. I saw a parallel between their full ripe beauty and Jennifer's way of dancing. She took the plums with thanks and an off-hand comment from which I inferred that she did not care for fruit. I told her of my strong response to *Speeds* and that my perception of the work was influenced by my most reliable "teacher" up until then, Johann Sebastian Bach.

During my first 3 years in New York, I frequently attended performances of Bach cantatas at a church on 65th Street and Central Park West. The musicians were first rate, the acoustics were excellent and the music nourished my mind, spirit and senses. I often pulled a 3×5 card from the back of the pew in front of me and drew images, usually of dancers, inspired by the music. I later learned that Jennifer had turned away from classical music after graduating from Juilliard where the canon dominates. Perhaps she understood my allusion, nonetheless, to the passion and form that flows through Bach's compositions.

I told Jennifer that I wanted to dance with her. She replied pragmatically, "Well, you know, I don't have a company." And I said, "Yes, but still . . ." The strength of *Speeds* had suggested to me that she could set off on her own path at any moment. Four months later, in October 1974, I became a founding member of her company, eventually named Jennifer Muller/The Works.

## Stretch

Our very first project as a company in 1974 was the setting of Jennifer's *Winter Pieces* (1973), with a new score composed by Burt Alcantara, her frequent collaborator. The work concerns dissolving relationships and has a strong psychoemotional tone. In directing rehearsals, Jennifer demanded and encouraged each of us to inhabit the choreography personally by connecting deeply with our selves. A highly effective director, she employed what was, in my experience, a unique rehearsal technique called "dialogue run-throughs." During a dialogue run-through each dancer speaks aloud their inner motivations while dancing the piece full out. Terrifying, this process also proved transformative, pushing us to take risks and increase our awareness. Keeping the improvisational dialogue going while fulfilling the choreographic demands for stamina, emotional credibility, and technical strength required mindfulness, commitment, and lung capacity. I found myself in unknown territory where kinetic and emotional energy merged.

Interestingly, this approach resulted in greater technical achievement. Jumps sprang higher, turns multiplied, and energy expanded as we threw ourselves into voicing our unwritten script. The process provided opportunities to plumb wells of longing and despair—a crucible from which I felt drained, cleansed and renewed. Working in this way stretched us as performers. Jennifer generally created her pieces at a level a bit beyond our current ability as dancers, so *stretch* became a familiar experience in working with her.

During my 15 years with The Works, the company performed in major theaters on four continents. I partnered with fantastically talented artists, learned invaluable life lessons, experienced sublimity, acquired sustainable work methods, developed a taste and aptitude for teaching both on tour and at home in New York, and eventually accepted the title of associate artistic director. The years brought many rewards and challenges. The hundreds of performances in Europe; the Middle East; and North, Central, and South America constituted a journey, both literal and figurative, that offered tremendous opportunities to grow as performers and as people.

The first 7 years of the company's existence were characterized by the excitement of standing ovations and steadily increasing strengths. We took great enjoyment in our work and often stayed after rehearsal to spend time together. We laughed often. Jennifer's directorial style included telling jokes and anecdotes in the midst of a hard-working rehearsal. The original company members were quite outspoken around the table and our group dynamics were colorful enough to make a credible television series.

## The Floating World

Jennifer modeled an infectious love and enthusiasm for travel. Our tours often took us overseas where we encountered a rich mixture of customs, cultures, and contrasting attitudes that influenced us as people and as artists. Languages, currency, foods, architecture, weather, landscapes, and people whirled past as we traveled from place to place. I called this experience "The Floating World." At the center, our work together on stage remained a constant. Enriched by our myriad experiences, our performing grew deeper and stronger. I discovered that to thrive on tour called for connecting with my colleagues onstage and off. As the company's reputation grew, the touring itinerary expanded. The panorama of cities, hotels, theaters, restaurants, and cultures taught me to cultivate inner space, adopt an affirmative attitude of adventure, and recognize the constancy of change. My sense of life expanded. My self-awareness deepened. I became a more resilient person and discovered that I carry my home within me.

## Appreciate Freedom

An experience that had a big effect on my perspective occurred at the start of a European tour. We were booked at Berlin's Akademie der Kunst. The wall still divided the city but bus tours to East Berlin were available. While West Berlin sizzled with activity, the streets on the other side of the wall were virtually empty. From the bus window, I saw a couple of desultory lines of people waiting outside dispensaries here and there. Their body language suggested fatigue, apathy, perhaps hopelessness. Faces seemed to turn away. A sense of isolation and constraint lay over the city like a leaden blanket.

A massive war memorial served as the halfway point and putative climax of the tour. We debarked and walked to the site. The monument was severe, heroic, grandiose, intended to intimidate, as if to say, "The system is strong; the individual is insignificant." During the return trip to West Berlin, I realized that I had taken for granted so many freedoms a U.S. citizen enjoys every day such as personal openness, the pursuit of happiness, social access, choice of career, even availability of groceries. I resolved to keep my eyes open from that day forward and appreciate these things.

## A Game Change

Starting in 1981, as U.S. dance companies became more expensive to present overseas and European countries began investing more in their own contemporary dance artists, we began to focus on fundraising at home. I became more involved in the office operations. My sense of capability grew as I helped to design brochures, write letters, organize fundraising events, and so forth, in addition to dancing. Dance companies, however, often resemble families: The director is like a parent and the dancers are like children who eventually grow up. I understood that Jennifer's choreographic career would have a longer arc than mine as a dancer in her company.

## On a Rock

One day in December 1988 while on winter holiday, I found myself sitting on a boulder in a bay on the coast of Itaparica, an island in Bahia, Brazil. The boulder was just large enough for me to sit on. I listened to the countless waves on every side rising and falling with little slaps and swooshing noises. The composite sound was like an enormous oceanic choir. Each wave spoke. The million voices, in their quiet-deafening way, each seemed to be saying: "Time to move on . . . move on . . . move on . . ."

For years relatives and friends had asked, "Have you thought about what you'll do after you stop dancing?" I countered, "Right now I *am* dancing; someday something else will happen." Someday had arrived. That spring, following our season at the Joyce Theater, I separated from the company, calling it a leave of absence. After 15 years up close with Jennifer, seeing her wrestle with the challenges of managing and directing, I did not envision myself starting a company of my own. Nor did I see another dance company that I wanted to join. I considered returning to acting or to visual art to find out what might happen. For a few months I picked up small walk-on roles in daytime television dramas.

Then one day the phone rang and, recommended by a Muller dancing partner (Holly Schiffer), I visited the University of California, Santa Barbara as a lecturer for winter quarter 1990. During that year, I also created commissions for four companies, including Jennifer's, and was invited to return to UC Santa Barbara. Twenty-two years later, I continue to choreograph and teach there, sustained by my passion for dance and art, still enthralled by the creative process, and curious about life. I have shown and sold my work as a visual artist. I have accepted the roles of vice chair of the Department of Theater and Dance, director of dance and artistic director of Santa Barbara Dance Theater, the department's professional company-in-residence. My wish for my students is that they discover their own curiosity, freedom, exuberance, and surrender through this medium. When I hear the words of my teachers flowing from me I recognize that I am a channel, a player in a generational game of telephone. I still teach the fall I learned when I was

13. In 2001, I paid homage to my early teachers in a dance piece entitled *Scrapbook* that began and ended with the spiral study from the first modern dance class I took with Norma. I now feel closer to understanding Henry Adams' statement: "*A teacher affects eternity; he can never tell where his influence stops.*"

## Spiral Time

One evening, while on tour with Jennifer, each of us around the dinner table described how he or she habitually envisioned the passage of time. Although none of us had ever discussed the topic before, everyone found that they indeed carried some kind of mental construct that gave time a shape. From childhood I have consistently viewed the flow of time as a modified spiral. Familiar markers on the calendar are revisited annually but each year brings new experiences that change the perspective and move the spiral along. Perhaps this will lead to a final, upward burst and an ecstatic surrender. Choreographically, that would work as a last gesture.

## Reference

Rainer, Y. (1965). "NO" to spectacle. *Tulane Drama Review, 10*(2), 178.

4

# Keep Your Knees Loose &
# Be Ready to Jump in Any Direction

## Darwin Prioleau

I was an avid skier in my early to mid-20s, when I had the opportunity to ski in Alta, Utah, one of the most challenging slopes in this country. I ventured to the top of a black diamond-level slope with my ski instructor. As I skied off the lift to position myself to descend the mountain, I froze. The slope looked a straight drop to me. My ski instructor encouraged me to go down, to no avail. Finally he said the magic words, "Just keep your knees loose and be ready to jump in any direction." (Coincidentally this phrase is a key component of African and jazz dance!) I was also a member of a dance company. Soon after this trip, the artistic director gave me an ultimatum to stop skiing or leave the company. My decision was easy. I loved skiing; I loved dancing more!

## What Could I Have Been Thinking?

At first glance, my journey may seem nontraditional. After all, traditionally, professional dancers have a performing career, eventually return to college to obtain their master's degree, and finally become university faculty, right? My experiences have encompassed everything from training in ballet, modern, and jazz, to dancing as a professional, and directing a small company in New York City. Additionally, I taught at studios and various colleges; chaired two dance departments; obtained my doctorate in educational policy, research, and administration in higher education; and finally, in my present position, served as dean for a unit of 15 departments. What dancer in her right mind would want to become a college administrator? Although I love what I do, I must admit that on occasion I ask myself: "What could I have been thinking?"

Every step has been germane to getting me where I am today as a person, a dance artist and an administrator. In retrospect, I consider my journey to be a pretty natural progression, but my trek has been anything but linear. I didn't stand at the ballet *barre* daydreaming of becoming a dean in higher education; more likely I daydreamed about becoming the sugar plum fairy or, at the very least, concentrated on finding the perfect *plié*. After all these years, finding the perfect *plié* has continued to elude me. I in no way mean to discourage those of you who wish to continue the search.

The bottom line is that I never considered becoming anything but a professional dancer, much to my parents' chagrin. They clearly felt that attending college was not optional. From a very young age, I studied with public school teachers who inspired me, and strong dance teachers who mentored me, working tirelessly to help me to prepare for my future. The majority of my teachers were men; I am grateful to them for their profound influence on my training and professional career. However, my confidence and determination were primarily fostered by three women, all of whom were in ballet: Florence Lessing, director of the New York Academy of Ballet in New York City; Olivia Rivers, an adjunct faculty at Bennett College as well as a soloist with the Greensboro Ballet Company in North Carolina; and Rosella Hightower, then director of the Centre de Danse in Cannes, France, and former premier ballerina with the New York City Ballet. Each of these women gave me a special gift. In an unwelcoming ballet world for black dancers, Olivia taught me that the only thing that ethnicity and incapability have in common is that they are both nouns. Rosella taught me that exquisite style can be more important than perfect technique.

Florence influenced me the most. Even in the beginning of our teacher–student relationship, I knew something about her was special. She epitomized the typical ballet mistress of the time, with her austere black bun at the nape of her neck; black leotard, tights, and slippers; and the requisite calf-length black skirt. Florence was strict. She had high expectations for all her students, both those who had the potential to be successful in the profession as well as those who did not. I remember her saying: "Everyone can and should dance, but not everyone can or should make a living from it." She understood the broader value of dance for those who were less talented and took their studies seriously, but she was dedicated to those of us who she felt had the fervor, tenacity, and potential to become professionals.

In many ways Florence Lessing was a dichotomy. A serious and exceptional classical ballet teacher, she possessed an earthiness that seemed at odds with the ethereal aesthetic of ballet. She insisted that we move as though we were "one with the music." She gave tortuously difficult, intricate, rhythmic petite allegros. She passionately emphasized that the grounded preparation was the secret to a stunning grand jeté. Something about her unusual imagery and her sometimes-unorthodox approach set her apart from my other ballet teachers. Indeed when teaching a jazz class, I often use imagery inspired by something Florence said. For example, usually my jazz dance students encounter difficulty understanding the concept of being grounded, erroneously believing that they simply need to bend their knees. Influenced by Florence, I often use the image of toddlers with heavy loads in their diapers. Inevitably eliciting laughter at first, the result is a kinesthetic and visual understanding of what being grounded means. Important in all forms of dance, understanding this concept is essential to executing vernacular-based jazz dance successfully.

No doubt her nontraditional approach was due to her nontraditional professional dance background. Florence moved like a gazelle, subtle but powerful. She repudiated the idea that in ballet power was the sole purview of male ballet dancers. The women in my class learned that power and grace were not mutually exclusive. She challenged us to find ourselves in our dancing, to celebrate our individuality and to push our boundaries. I knew that Florence was the primary dance partner to the famous Jack Cole; what I didn't know was that Jack Cole was considered by many to be the father of jazz dance. This indirect link between Jack Cole and Florence's teaching would years later become part of my jazz connection.

## It Is What It Is!

My understanding of the power of dance expanded after attending my first Alvin Ailey American Dance Theatre concert. I particularly remember a duet performed by Judith Jamison and Miguel Godreau. I watched amazed as a small, wiry male and a tall, long-limbed woman danced together with such beauty, intensity, and animalistic power. I remember hairs standing up on the back of my neck. I knew that I wanted to immerse myself in the essence of the Ailey tradition. I was determined to audition and receive a scholarship and apprenticeship at the Ailey School. I accomplished my mission.

My transition from ballet to modern at the Ailey School was not difficult. The classical modern styles taught there, especially the structure and clarity of the Horton technique, lent themselves easily to my classically trained body. However, tackling jazz was more challenging. Jazz dance requires the *aesthetic of cool*, a term coined by art historian Robert Ferris Thompson (1966) to illuminate one of the distinct traits of African dance. I believe Pepsi Bethel and Ed Kresley embodied this essential component of jazz. Their quick rhythmic footwork and sense of weightiness had an urgency and coolness that was both exciting and intimidating. I always felt I was behind a quarter beat in their classes. I felt anything but cool. Where they were grounded I was elevated; where they looked relaxed I looked uptight; where they attacked movement from a parallel stance I struggled to turn in my hard-won turnout. In my mind, I felt that my purpose in jazz class was to amuse the other dancers. I felt that as a dancer I needed to conquer jazz, when in reality I simply needed to conquer the fear of allowing myself to actuate my own artistry. I needed to find my "personal cool." In order to succeed, I had to let it happen, instead of trying to make it happen. Of course, practice and observing others helped. I ultimately improved my execution of jazz. I could dance jazz but I was not a "jazz" dancer.

Most of my journeys have had moments when I felt lost. Often, I had all the pieces of the puzzle, but how they fit together was an enigma. I found myself stuck at that point in my jazz dance travels. I kept looking for the right direction. Years later I learned no "right" direction existed. Pepsi Bethel often would say: "It is what it is." I thought, at the time, that he meant that the movement could only be done one way, the right way. However, after many years of researching jazz as an American vernacular, I now believe his statement means that authentic jazz is what it is at any moment in time; it is constantly changing based on the people and the situation at hand. I am uncertain whether or not this is what he meant. I do know that my understanding of his phrase has stayed with me and guided me through the decades, helping me to maintain integrity in what I teach, and even to embrace change in my personal and professional life. It is what it is.

Although I worked with many jazz teachers in New York City over the years, I found my voice dancing with the Nat Horne Dance Company in the late 1970s and early 1980s. Horne, a jazz teacher at the Ailey School, left to start his own dance company and school, purchasing a theater on Theatre Row off Broadway. Dancing with his company gave me the opportunity to use all my dance training. I had taken his classes when I was at Ailey and his style felt right for me. There I was able to be grounded, and use the style and quick footwork I learned from Bethel and Kresley, the musicality I gained from Lessing, and the vocabulary and capacity for swift changes of direction I took from Horne. My ballet partnering experience and modern dance training allowed me to cross styles and demonstrate versatility; I eventually became Horne's dance partner, and a featured dancer in his company. This experience and exposure led to many lucrative opportunities, including well-paid commercial work, "pick-up work" with a variety of dance companies, and eventually my first college teaching position.

## Always Know the Origin

While dancing professionally in New York City I taught at different places; however, I primarily taught at the 92nd Street Y and The Door. The Door, under the auspice of The International Center for Integrative Studies, was an experimental center dedicated to servicing inner-city, at-risk youth between the ages of 13 and 18 years. These two programs epitomized opposite sides of the spectrum. While trained dancers took my classes at the 92nd Street Y, I found teaching at The Door was much more challenging. Many of the young people I taught possessed a natural talent for movement, but were not trained as dancers. They were hungry and willing to attempt anything. The more I challenged them, the more determined they became. I have never observed this level of rapid growth in young dancers. I could write a full chapter about my experiences at The Door; however, I want to acknowledge how much I learned about myself from these students. I realized that if I wanted to keep pace with their inquisitive minds and physical talents, I needed to expand my dance knowledge beyond technique. I was particularly interested in acquiring a deeper understanding of the dancing body and the aesthetics of modern dance. After some research and several recommendations from my mentors, I was encouraged to study with three capable dance masters in New York City: Ernestine Stodelle, Andre Bernard, and Nada Diachenko. These individuals taught at various schools, but had one common denominator. They all taught at New York University (NYU). Under their tutelage, I eventually completed my master's of arts in dance and dance education at NYU.

I acquired my first job in higher education almost by mistake. I was just about to complete my master's degree. Through Nat Horne, I received an invitation to teach jazz dance master classes at Southern Methodist University in Dallas, Texas. The chair of the Dance Department at the time, Toni Beck, observed me teach. From her chair, she began to perform the isolations I gave to the class. Afterward she told me how excited she was that I was teaching Matt Mattox isolations. She had danced with Matt when he worked in New York City. I was embarrassed to admit that I did not know that I was teaching Matt Mattox's work. Beck was ecstatic about the possibilities of her students studying his jazz style. By the end of the week, I was offered a tenure-track position with a bonus of a 2-year reduction in time to secure tenure. I sublet my New York City apartment and 3 months later I was living in Dallas, which was probably the last place I thought I would ever be living. However, one has to be able to adapt in this field. I considered the move temporary, but was intrigued by the opportunity to develop a serious jazz component in a program that, at that time, was known for classical ballet and Graham modern technique.

Clearly, I needed firsthand experience with Matt Mattox if I was to continue teaching some of his style. My family taught me about the importance of personal ethics. My grandparents and parents lived through times when the works and ideas of black artists, inventors, and scientists had been consistently appropriated by their white counterparts, who then presented the work as their own, often bastardized. Similarly, for me, any kind of misappropriation of a specific style or cultural movement without at least an acknowledgment of the source is unconscionable. Doing so would be akin to stealing part of the "soul" of an individual or peoples. I learned from this experience and, supported by my background, the importance of always, and I mean always, making sure that you know the origin of anything you learn and especially teach.

## Dancer for the Ages

The next leg of my journey took me to France. I spent the subsequent three summers following Matt Mattox from Paris to Les Arc, to Perpignan and every city in between. I had the opportunity to work closely with him. His work was physically and intellectually challenging. He was very detailed about every movement. Matt never referred to what he taught as jazz, he described his work as "freestyle." Watching him dance was like watching a slender but muscularly defined leopard glide through space. His physical prowess seemed to dominate even the most skilled professional dancers in class, most of whom were 30 to 40 years his junior. I learned an important lesson regarding preconceptions about dance ability in relation to age. This lesson continues to infuse my principles as an artist and as an administrator.

Matt understood at a deep level the nuances and variety of undercurrents in dance, whereas others viewed only a vast undifferentiated sea of movement. Even his seemingly mechanical series of intricate body isolations were seamless and fluid if done correctly. His linking of the cerebral and the kinesthetic was pure artistry. In his class I usually found myself trying to execute such feats as legato hip rhythms, along with staccato arms all the while traveling forward with syncopated leg movements. Upon first observance, the different phrases that Matt created may seem coincidental or simply chance occurrences. In reality, they were anything but accidental. They were well-conceived dialects of challenging movement that he made look easy.

Over the years I have changed the way I teach jazz, yet I continue to teach much of Matt's isolation series, finding his style to be a wonderful catalyst for mind–body connections. What I took from him was considerably deeper than movement or style. I learned how to connect the challenges embodied in his work with the challenges embodied in life. I performed his movements well, but, more importantly, I grasped the intellectual problem-solving properties of what and how he taught. As I moved from dancer and professor to department chair and eventually to dean of a school, Matt continued to encourage me. He not only supported me, he never questioned the sanity of my choices. In fact, he applauded each step in my journey and saw my progression as a powerful move forward for the art form. I am grateful for his tutelage as a teacher and choreographer, and I feel blessed that Matt supported my move into unchartered territory.

## Watch Where You Are Going or You Might Land in a Place that You Do Not Recognize

Before beginning this section, I want to explain my use of the words "deanery" and "chairdom." I coined these words to help me keep things in perspective. My experiences have shown me the direct correlation between the ability to keep a sense of humor, and the ability to maintain my sanity while acting as a chair or a dean.

The responsibility of chairdom is thrust upon some faculty; others gladly embrace the step as a natural progression in their careers. If you are one of the former individuals I have some important advice for you—watch where you are going, or like Alice in Wonderland, you might land in a place that you do not recognize. That unrecognizable place may be your very own department. The road to becoming a department head from full-time faculty status can be precarious, definitely not made for those who are not able or eager to navigate through an exciting but often frustrating academic maze. Fortunately, those individuals who actually want to be chairs believe they can make a difference. I put myself in that category. I neither encourage nor discourage those who see chairdom as part of their future journey; however, I strongly recommend to anyone considering this academic career move to first view the big picture through the widest lens possible. In my travels I have found that seeing the big picture (warts and all) is essential to achieving success. Also, be aware that the same verve and tenacity that you brought to your dance artistry often will be required as chair. The tricky part is figuring out when and how to use these powers for the good of the whole.

I have chaired two dance programs, the first at Kent State University and the second was at my present institution, The College of Brockport, State University of New York. Both institutions afforded me the opportunity to work with a cadre of talented dance faculty who were committed to teaching and maintaining their professional profile. I was the first dance chair hired through a national search process at each institution and both dance programs were going through a major transition at the time of my hire. Finally, Kent and Brockport are also both state-affiliated public institutions. Here the similarities end; Kent and Brockport are vastly different in size, focus, academic intent, demographics, and institutional structure. Although both institutions recently had undergone the restructuring of their academic units, their dance programs were affected in different ways. The dance program at Kent State went from being housed in a large college to being housed in a small college with similar disciplines. The Brockport Dance Department went from being housed in a small school to being housed in a large school with wide-ranging disciplines.

I was unprepared for the rather perplexing and almost schizophrenic nature of chairdom. A former provost once told me that chairs are "first among faculty." What at first seemed to me to be a rather nebulous phrase, became clear later through my own chairdom experiences. The faculty expected me to act as their four-star general who, at a moment's notice, would push forward to the front line to obtain and protect all that they perceived to be rightfully theirs. The deans expected me to be savvier about the nuances of academic policy and the institutional strategic plan than regular faculty. Therefore, with a schizophrenic feel to implementation, my job was to support the needs of the faculty while simultaneously supporting the initiatives of the administration, even when the two were in contention. Hence, I came to the conclusion that the phrase "first among faculty" should be instead *super faculty*. To be truthful, I may have presented this in a slightly exaggerated fashion, but I still stand behind my previous statement regarding the "schizophrenic nature of the position."

What is important is that I accepted these chair positions not knowing that I was walking into situations fraught with trials and tribulations. The most significant difference was the institutional culture. The challenge was to find an approach that would enable us together to successfully navigate these terrains. I found that the process of solving the riddle of institutional culture to be similar to solving an intricate crossword puzzle; once you find the key answers the rest will begin to fall into place. I drew inspiration from my experiences and challenges as a dance artist. I saw this as an opportunity to hone my previously developed skills and learn new ones pertinent to my success in the prevailing culture. In each case, I strove to make a difference. I found the experience to be both educational and gratifying.

## When You Come to a Fork in the Road, Take It

My journey to becoming a dean was the most difficult of my academic career. When the opportunity was presented, I was unsure whether I wanted to go down this road. The position was founding dean of the School of The Arts, Humanities and Social Sciences at the College of Brockport with 15 departmental units. Several faculty members nominated me, and others encouraged me to apply. I knew that I wanted to become a dean at some point in my career; however, my ideal position was dean of a school or college of the arts. Being the dean of a unit that included disciplines outside of the arts never occurred to me.

Previously, I had always been an external candidate for positions. Consequently, I was ill equipped for the difference between the interview dynamics for an internal as opposed to an external candidate. In this situation, the old idiom, "familiarity breeds contempt," could more appropriately be worded "perceived familiarity breeds contempt." As a black female dance artist, navigating the traditional culture of higher education often has been a trying, sometimes frustrating, and occasionally amusing experience. I found the interview process for the dean position to be trying and frustrating, but never amusing. Let me be perfectly clear: Many individuals from all levels of the academy encouraged and supported me during this process. Without them, I most likely would not have considered applying for or accepting this position. I have always found having an energetic support system when antagonists are nipping at your heels most helpful.

As dancers, the moving body stands at the center of our world. If one is to believe that movement has meaning, then the body is the instrument through which that meaning is expressed. As various groups at the college interviewed me, I used this knowledge. The ability to read the body language of those in attendance at each meeting helped to prepare me for their questions. The most memorable question was, and I quote, "What makes you think that someone who is a dancer could possibly evaluate 'real' scholarship?" I must admit that this question caught me by surprise. I was stunned by the blatant insult, not only to me but also to my entire field. But most significantly, the question reflected the ignorance, lack of tact, and basic good manners of the individual who asked it. Even his peers appeared appalled. How I answered this question is less important than how I responded. I swayed on my toes just a little, gained my balance almost immediately, and maintained my "personal cool." I knew at that moment that I could handle anything. However, the question remained: Did I want to take on this titanic challenge or remain as chair of the dance department? I had put much time and effort into moving this department forward to gain a national reputation. Once again, I was at a fork in the road on my journey. Yogi Berra was quoted as saying, "When you come to a fork in the road, take it." I did.

I believe that individuals must use all of their resources and all of their life and professional experiences in order to succeed. I often use the metaphor of the "purple velvet bag" to help reassure graduating seniors that they have learned much during their college experience and are prepared to move forward. I encourage them to keep all that they have learned and accomplished in their personal metaphoric purple velvet bag. Although they may not use everything they have learned immediately, they will be able to pull out many of these treasures when they most need them. As a dancer and as a person I have had to face many situations where my abilities were questioned; when I had to remain strong even though I felt my confidence dwindling; when I had to work with people whom I would never want to have as friends; and when I was able to accomplish something so amazing that I surprised even myself. These are all treasures that I have kept in my purple velvet bag over the years. Some of those treasures might stay in the bag for decades, others I pull out daily. They have all been collected from lessons learned, obstacles surmounted, and the wise words of those who have helped me along my journey. I hope to find many more treasures. With many riches in my purple velvet bag, I know for sure that if I keep my knees loose, I will be ready to jump in any direction.

## Reference

Thompson, R.F. (1966). An aesthetic of cool: West African dance. *African Forum*, 2(2), 89.

## 5

# "Just Do Something, Anything!"

## David Leventhal

It is 1997 and Mark Morris stands in the middle of a large sunlit studio at 890 Broadway in New York City surrounded by his dancers, rehearsing one of his classic pieces, *Gloria* (1981), set to Vivaldi's eponymous Mass. The dancers are dancing, but they are not, according to their boss, committing to anything. Long curls cascade down over his wide shoulders as he crouches down on the floor, sandals squeaking with strain, muscled knees protruding through his long shorts. He implores his company to dance the way he always did—fully, with the uncanny combination of weighted intention and beguiling spontaneity. "Do something, anything!" he pleads. The dancers are doing something, of course, but to Mark, their force seems to be diminished by their own self-conscious reticence.

At the time of this event, one of my first and strongest memories of my 14-year career with Mark Morris and his group, I was something of an outsider. Several Morris pieces require extra dancers to supplement the regular company, and I was an understudy for one—*L'Allegro, Il Penseroso ed il Moderato* (1988). I had not had much exposure to Mark or his choreographic process, so I was eager to learn more about how he worked with his dancers. My surreptitious peek into company rehearsal that day confirmed my developing comprehension that this was a man who had no patience for apathy, and no time for inertia.

Fourteen years later, I am sitting in a studio in Charlotte, North Carolina, across from a man in his late 70s whom I will call Bill. I am facilitating a workshop for teachers who want to do what my colleagues John Heginbotham,

Misty Owens, and I started doing 10 years ago at the Mark Morris Dance Center—teaching specially designed dance classes for people with Parkinson's disease (PD). Parkinson's poses many challenges, but among them, it increases the difficulty for people to initiate movement spontaneously. The neurodegenerative disorder, caused by the death of dopamine-producing cells in the substantia nigra, also can make a person's movements smaller and slower (or, in the case of freezing, entirely nonexistent), can cause a resting tremor, and can manifest a lack of postural stability resulting in a stoop, shuffling gait and greater risk for falling. Dance for PD, as our dance program is known, began at the urging of Brooklyn Parkinson Group's executive director Olie Westheimer. The program has found a welcoming home at the Mark Morris Dance Center, where we encourage people with PD to use their imaginations in the service of graceful, musical movement.

On this particular day in Charlotte, Bill's face is expressionless as he watches me lead a sweeping *port de bras* that engages the arms, back, and head. As we begin a foot exercise, I can see him try to move his left leg into a *tendu*, but just as he seems to process the command, his wife interrupts him: "Watch him, do what he's doing. Come on, move your leg out." The man is flummoxed by the extra spousal coaching, and freezes again, unable to move. Too many cues are going on and like a circuit on overload, the man's body is unable to take the next step. I encourage him softly: "It doesn't have to be the same leg, just reach toward me. Try to do something; anything is going to be great."

Try to do something, anything. As a dancer in Mark's company, I struggled throughout my career to initiate a choreographer's difficult, idiosyncratic movement in a fluid, spontaneous, and personalized way. Now the same strategies that I used to dig deeper into the work and follow my choreographer's demands—internalizing the music, using the imagination, dancing with others, exploring one's inner life—prove incredibly valuable to those who must follow the frustrating and unpredictable dictates of a movement disorder. Our dancers with PD, with the right combination of instruction, music, inspiration, and support, find that the challenges they often confront on the street dissipate in the safe and positive environment of the dance studio.

Mark's imploration is, quite simply, what dance is about. And I believe the Cartesian corollary—I do, therefore I am—is the great theatrical vindication that can frame a dancer's entire identity. Dance is action, and dancers do. In a dancer's hands, inert stillness becomes loaded with potential energy—something is always about to happen. In *L'Allegro*, for example, which came to be one of my favorite dances in the repertory, I danced the role of the lark, which appears as a symbol of bright, day-time pleasures in contrast to Il Penseroso's nightingale. Technically, because the solo is constructed entirely of balances, runs, jumps and on-a-dime turns, the Lark dance scared the daylights out of me at every performance. Artistically, the challenge was simply to be, not act, avian and as birds do, oscillate constantly between complete stillness and hyper-frenetic movement. As I got older, I played more with the moments of stillness, elongating them, experiencing them as a suspension of movement, not as a locked freeze as I did when I was younger. The stillness of my suspended lark informed and highlighted the flurry of activity that followed, which I think (and hope) was what Mark intended when he choreographed the dance. By having the dancer constantly stop and start throughout, he not only created avian verisimilitude, but also playfully unpacked and exposed the crux of a dancer's alchemical ability.

For me, whether ornithological or not, all dance is the conversation between action and controlled stillness, and dancers train to be able to initiate difficult movement from stillness with grace and flow. Consequently, when you put people with PD in a room with professional dancers, a meaningful exchange of information occurs. Indeed our students with PD tell us, in unequivocal terms, that when they are in class, they are able to do things that they cannot ordinarily do at home.

"When I first heard of this group I was so touched and surprised that anyone would think of something so magnificent and drastic as trying to teach all of us slowpokes to dance," wrote a student in one of the Oakland Dance for PD classes (our program has been a model for classes in more than 50 other communities in seven countries). "What a marvel. I had pretty much settled into my life as a wallflower. If there is anything that sidelines you, exacerbates your sense of constriction and inhibition it is Parkinson's. If there is anything that calls for expression, demonstration, drama, movement, expression and liveliness it is dance." Drama, movement, expression—these were the things Mark, crouching in the middle of the studio, begged his dance company to manifest.

I was partly drawn to Mark's work because of this powerful expressive force. He sublimely captures a panoply of moods and emotions embodied in an uncomplicated movement vocabulary and unpretentious aesthetic. But his sensitivity and love of music sealed the deal. I always felt like an anomaly—a boy growing up in the 1980s preferring classical music to rock or pop. I was an amateur musician (piano), but a very serious listener. To me, music was the best thing about the ballet classes I took as a young boy at Boston Ballet, and music has always sustained me in dance and in life.

In the Dance for PD classes, my colleagues and I try to create a comfortable and nourishing place where the elements of drama, movement, and expression are always strongly informed by music, and where music can play the same role for our participants (blood, pulse, and inspiration) as in my own artistic journey. Music seems the key to two particularly important doors for dancers and people with PD. Music, through rhythm, creates a unified understanding of time and duration, a template for our choreography. For people moving at all speeds and ranges of slowness, music provides a welcome friend, judge, and guide. "Here, do this now and for this long." When you are done, the reward feels good—the internal reward we get for being on the beat, a reward that we are probably biologically wired to desire and attain. But I also believe music is the most immediate path to the imagination. When we hear something, especially a tune we know, our memories, senses and imaginative powers awaken, telling us why and how to move. Dancers have many techniques for initiating movement, but this constant invocation of the imagination is the one that sets artists apart from technicians, and allows people with PD to do things in a dance class that they may not be able to do in a session with a therapist. Music dances in miraculous ways but is just sound. The transubstantiation of that music into action happens as the imagination guides the body to move. I feel particularly honored to share this imagination in action with our Parkinson's students, and they respond with a level of engagement at total odds with what their lives have handed them.

Just as Mark does for his dancers in rehearsal, John, Misty, and I use imagination and imagery to help our students harness an aesthetic objective in the service of action. But in most other ways, our teaching approach, and the nature of power and relationships in the studio, is completely different from the experience of being a dancer in Mark's company. Many choreographers (and playwrights, among others) depend primarily on others to satisfy and carry out their visions. I was an individual, with my own training, artistic voice, and imaginative interpretation, but I was also a piece of animated clay, ready to be formed into whatever shape Mark wanted. By necessity, the hierarchy of creator to interpreter in Mark's company was always clear to me—I was there to serve his vision. For some this type of hierarchy can trickle down into training as well—many teachers see class as a unidirectional platform from which they spread wisdom to hungry disciples.

In the world of Dance for PD, by choice, mission, and necessity, ours is a nonhierarchical learning environment in which I learn as much from the students with PD as the students learn from me. Certainly we are there to provide a certain knowledge base and source of inspiration for our students, but ours is a class of symbiotic learners. We dance in a circle together; we facilitate improvisation, giving creative power to our students; and we dance with our students rather than stepping back and watching them perform for us. We listen to their feedback—what they want in the class—and adapt our teaching to suit their changing needs and interests. As we explore movement together, without the traditional teacher-student dynamic, the concept of hierarchy falls away.

As Dance for PD restructures traditional teacher–student relationships in the studio, the program also changes our understanding of the role of dance in our lives and our society. This shift happened for me at a very personal level, before I was aware of the broader ramifications. I loved almost every minute of my performing career, but I realized after a few years in Mark's company that being a professional dancer requires a cloistered inner focus that I found less and less inviting. Although Mark's work always felt meaningful and rewarding to do, I started to have trouble finding and maintaining a sense of lasting purpose. On many days, training for hours, fulfilling the vision of a master choreographer, and bringing joy to thousands of strangers in dark theaters was enough. On some days, it was not. Before I was even aware of this sensation, Olie Westheimer had already approached the Mark Morris Dance Group (MMDG) on a hunch that a real dance class, taught by professional dancers, might have tangible benefits for people with PD, and I had already started teaching the Parkinson's class. I got involved with the program initially by accident rather than through a personal quest for meaning. My colleague John Heginbotham, who was originally chosen to teach the Parkinson's class, had to leave town for a family emergency, and I filled in for him. Even on that first day, I found a level of sincerity and strength of purpose that has only expanded as the program has grown far beyond our expectations.

People in our classes often take me aside, look directly into my eyes, and thank me for the work that we do with the Parkinson's community. "Thank you for sharing your time with us," they say. "To think that professional dancers would want to spend their time teaching us is so touching." I do not actually know how to respond because the pleasure and honor is mine. I feel grateful to be able to offer something that so many people in society do not value—dance making and dance teaching—and present dance and music to a population of people who value so profoundly what we have to share. This makes me feel good, and speaks to the sense of purpose that I feel teaching this population.

Within my personal transformation and this encouraging community response, I see a radical and potentially transformative direction for the dance world at a time when a new direction is most needed. By accident rather than by strategic intent, programs like Dance for PD are quietly participating in reframing the role of the arts in our society, and in doing so, engaging dance companies in missions that go beyond the original goal of presenting the works of creative and interpretive professionals to a specialized, elite niche of dance viewers. Dance for PD extends the reach of a single artist and artistic organization into new local and international communities, and into other fields like health care and scientific research.

Such progressive globalization brings plurality and diversity to the company's mission, broadens the discourse about the art form, and suggests a paradigm shift for what being a dancer, choreographer, and dance company means in the 21st century. Our inner sanctum is broadening.

I am not being an alarmist when I state that the professional concert dance world in which I have lived and worked is in crisis. Ticket sales are down, and audiences are getting older. Budgets—already meager—are getting slashed. Merce Cunningham is dead, Christopher Wheeldon abandoned his own company, and the Mikhailovsky Theater in St. Petersburg is run by a banana magnate. Mark turned 55 this year, his company celebrating 30 years—a remarkable achievement. Where is the next 25-year-old modern dance choreographer who will have his trajectory? Is that kind of trajectory even possible in this age of Facebook, YouTube, Twitter, and the Tea Party? What is the dance world going to do next so that our art form stays relevant?

Certainly we need to continue to nurture and celebrate choreographers and dancers who provide, at least for me, a welcome antidote to our anti-poetic, arts-phobic, late-capitalistic society. But just as our world has become more interconnected, so the institutions and disciplines that we have worked so hard to delineate, isolate, and refine need to converge to find opportunities for broader relevance and more creative exchange. Researchers need to listen to novelists; doctors should talk with dancers; musicians and neuroscientists should have lunch more often. The arts and artists can provide a much-needed anodyne and escape from pain or reality—and our dancers with PD understand this more completely than most—but the arts also can foster initiatives that present artistic practice as an essential response to society's needs. This redefines our purpose and is our call to action.

PD provides one clear point of convergence. As we have seen in Brooklyn, and wherever the Dance for PD program has taken root, training and thinking like a dancer seems to help people with PD rediscover a sense of grace, confidence, and physical agency that threatens to fall away. We do not talk about symptoms in our classes, or choreograph movements that address specific symptoms. If you were given the task of sitting in a lab and coming up with something that seemed to address almost all of the Parkinsonian concerns (balance, flexibility, coordination, rhythm, sequencing, initiation, and social inclusion) you would be hard-pressed to find something better than dance. Here I mean dance in the most general sense; ballet, modern, tap, jazz, kathak, flamenco, and ballroom dancing have different vocabularies but share an efficacy with this population.

For people with PD, dance changes things in small but significant ways. One of our students in Berkeley tells the story of using dance as a way to initiate his way toward the checkout counter in the grocery store. He felt himself slowing down, so instead of thinking of walking forward, he put himself into the role of choreographer, and transformed the path ahead into a choreographic task. He made a dance toward the register. One of our Brooklyn students fell in love with tap dance, and started to study privately with Misty Owens, while using some of the tap vocabulary to make his way out of bed in the middle of the night. Heel, toe, go! A woman in our Brooklyn group found herself able to dance for hours at a wedding—something she had not felt comfortable doing—because she had the confidence that comes from regular dance training. And a woman in a London Parkinson's dance class relayed how the *port de bras* practice she had done in her classes allowed her to have the confidence to reach a shelf in her kitchen that had been off limits for years.

The close relationship between the art of dancing and the reality of this movement disorder makes people start to sit up and take notice. Doctors refer people to our classes because they see the positive effects of arts-based interventions on their patients and the patients' partners and families (we invite spouses, partners, and care partners to the class). Neuroscience and social science researchers see both the disease itself and our art form as a window into understanding how the brain works, and are in the early stages of figuring out what to study and how. The art form that had drawn me in so strongly but had left me hungry for greater relevance, significance, and sense of social action has been transformed in my own mind into a gateway, a keystone, and a mode of transformation. We dancers, the lowly black sheep of the performing and visual arts family, have something valuable to say and to offer, and mother Terpsichore is not the only one listening.

One area of particular interest to me, and I hope to neuroscientists, is how dancers learn movement and execute complicated sequences that seem natural and automatic. This phenomenon elicits audiences around the world to ask us how we remember all those steps (and makes me want to know how pianists can play tens of thousands of notes by memory during a 2-hour concert). This phenomenon is of considerable interest to people with PD because those very movements that once were automatic—tying a shoe, getting out of a chair, taking a step—become less so. Each time someone with PD initiates a movement, he or she has to think about every step in order to execute the movement fully, no matter how familiar the sequence once was. As the disease progresses, more and more external cues (music, voice, a line on the floor) are needed to prevent freezing or inertia. Dancers train to do steps without thinking about each element, relying on what we call "muscle memory" (although there is no such thing—muscle memory happens only as an ingrained pattern in the brain). Dancers are particularly adept at converting new information into stored movement patterns that can be consistently replicated. We hope that this process gets shared to some degree in our classes. What about our training specifically (aside from time, repetition, and pleading choreographers) allows us to manifest this storage and recall so well, and what we can learn from this exploration that might help us guide our dancers with PD even more effectively? I have posed these questions to my scientist acquaintances and am waiting to hear back.

Even as we converge to share ideas and perspectives, Daniel Glaser, Wellcome Trust's head of special projects in public engagement in London, reminds us that divergence allows us to do our best work. We want to come together, exchange, and then go back to our respective areas of distinctive competence. Doctors should not be teaching dance, and dancers are not medical professionals. I believe we need to trust the respective power of our own fields to convey value to society without those fields becoming diluted. An arts experience loses force when medicalized; sometimes you need a pill, not a *plié*. But we can most certainly see our field and ourselves as important partners in providing a more fulfilling quality of life to people in our communities—and in society at large.

The most important work that happens in a Dance for PD class is the creation of an active, engaged community, a community that has become my new family. In addition to the professional communities that engage with Dance for PD as a platform, model, or laboratory, dozens of communities of people with PD now take charge of their lives and approach challenges as dancers do—creatively, musically, collaboratively. PD can make people apathetic, and getting up and out of the house to do something—anything— can seem like an impossible task. So they become more isolated, and more passive. No matter what your walk of life or sense of power before PD, the disease can rob you of your agency to do anything. For spouses, partners, and care partners, this can be particularly difficult.

Enter the dance class, a naturally inviting community that makes you feel welcome, asks you to interact with artists and peers, and turns everyone into a guide and mentor. Of the many activities available to people with PD, dance classes seem to have some of the highest level of what researchers and therapists call adherence—stick-to-it-iveness. People try dance and they come back, again and again. PD dance students bond with each other and with us teachers, and form a community where small individual gains in physical confidence and a sense of joy add up to a sense of mutual achievement. One person is as powerful as the whole. You see this when 45 people with PD strut their way across our Brooklyn studios smiling, swinging, and clapping. Then each member of that community takes the positive spirit and sense of achievement with them when they leave. From one to many and back to one, a beautifully simple formula.

This transformation is no less true for spouses, partners, and care partners. One wrote to me:

My husband was recently diagnosed with Parkinson's. It has been a roller coaster ride of emotions for us with all there is to learn about, the physical changes, and the emotional ones as well. It has not been an easy task for us thus far. However, I feel that being able to experience the class you shared, the participants (those with and without Parkinson's) and your spirit was so enlightening to me. I walked out of the class feeling such a sense of empowerment and peace. I was able to connect with some of the participants who were so compassionate about Parkinson's and my life and what we all go through together that I didn't feel so alone anymore.

Essentially, the powerful humanizing force of communal activity, a key objective of the Dance for PD program, is Mark Morris' artistic vision. Informed by folk dancing as a young person, Mark has a well-honed ability to evoke and celebrate the power of a community through his dances. He would not have imagined 30 years ago how pluralistically this vision has played out among a community so hungry for group empowerment. If the MMDG is the rarified, carefully produced representation of Mark's vision, Dance for PD is a piece of that vision extended to everyone else—the praxis.

The group's praxis is also my own. My mission did not begin with a well-developed theory or philosophy, or a community-centric vision as clear and steady as Mark's—just an aptitude for dance and a feeling that my professional life needed a clearer sense of purpose and a path toward service, that despite having such success as a professional dancer, I still felt a personal void. That void, fertilized by accumulating experiences with students with PD in our Brooklyn class, transformed into a journey toward something new and unexpected, a journey that was finally lending significant personal and lasting meaning to my professional calling, which had been wholly in the realm of poiesis—art for art's sake.

In the case of Dance for PD, poiesis and praxis do not merely coexist amicably side by side, separately but equally. They infiltrate and inform one another. Dance for PD students in Brooklyn come to see MMDG performances and then learn sections of the dances they have seen in class the following week. For me, this is one of the most satisfying aspects of the program, the part that embraces our dancers with PD as members of the larger artistic community symbolized by the bricks and mortar of the dance center. I always loved performing, for strangers, for friends, for family, but being able to travel seamlessly between the stage and the Dance for PD class, sharing the work of a living artist with a population that is fighting to live artfully, created a circle in my life where there had once been a horseshoe. I always loved knowing that our students with PD were in the audience, enjoying the performance even more because their brains were doing the dances along with us as they watched. This model of exchange thrives wherever possible—in Berkeley, Washington, and London—and serves to deepen the sense of inclusion and the falling away of disease and patienthood.

The performing arts can be, in themselves, transformative calls to action, but in 21st-century society, we tend to leave the theater and go home to ponder, blog, and wait for the next event. Just as you might after a good performance, people leave a Dance for PD class with a new perspective and a renewed sense of optimism about themselves and about their world. But more than that, participants come to see themselves as part of a vibrant and sustained community of engagement. Just as teaching these classes allows me to find personal meaning and value in what was once a rather cloistered existence, so these classes allow persons with PD to break out of individual pockets of isolation and return to the world. Connecting as dancers and students, they find that their disease is part of them, but that it does not own them.

Our society does not know how to place value on the powerful effects of this kind of community. The value cannot be measured in financial terms—yet. But Dance for PD serves as a reminder that dance and music have the potential to build communities of strength, exploration, and possibility. The program tells us, loudly, that dancers have a gift and a responsibility to serve as agents of transformation, not necessarily by executing brilliant performances, or by creating dances with political messages, or by performing to raise money for causes, or by devoting themselves in common, as Virgil Thomson once wrote, to a nonmaterialistic end—although these activities are all important. We can serve broader society simply by sharing with others our deep knowledge of movement and the joy that we feel when we move. People with PD are a perfect natural constituency, but dozens, perhaps hundreds of other communities deserve and yearn for what dancers can share with them.

This call to action may seem like a lot to ask of dancers, who are often already overwhelmed by the brutal demands of professional life. After all, many of us humbly serve choreographers who push us harder, audiences who expect more, and colleagues who rely on us to carry and support them. This call to action may be even more to expect of dance companies, who are struggling just to make ends meet. But without broadening the often isolated and isolating view of a professional life, we fail to recognize the power that we have to do something (anything!) that is our special gift and therefore our special responsibility. At the end of the day, we dancers have a place at the table as visionaries, community leaders, guides, and agents of social change.

People sometimes raise an eyebrow when they learn that I left my high-level performance career with one of the world's most respected modern dance companies to devote my energy to working with the PD community.

In addition to teaching, I manage the program's international expansion, train and nurture teachers, and create collaborative partnerships to sustain classes in other cities. Strangely, people used to raise the other eyebrow when I told them I was a dancer. They always wanted to know what I was going to do next, as if dancing were a hobby or a phase. This contradictory and infuriating eyebrow lifting seems to get at something restless, ephemeral, and unpredictable about my life and identity. But I trained to know everything and also to know nothing of what I would do next. I thrive on rehearsed spontaneity, and I have spent my professional life getting comfortable with that spontaneity. At a time in my career when I yearned for something deeper, I followed a new path—opened up to me by chance—and just kept moving. I believe stillness is all about the potential of what is to come; movement is a dancer's only currency. My time to share that currency and help people regain momentum is now. You will know when it is your turn.

# 6

# To Be a Lifer

## Falling to Flight

John-Mario Sevilla

### Another Lapse

Just the other day, the inevitable question bubbled up in conversation with a chatty cab driver. A policeman on Shelter Island later stopped me for speeding—I was trying not to miss the last ferry—and he too raised the query. Before that, the Home Depot paint salesman as well as the chiropractor at my gym posed the same interrogative: "What do you do?"

Each time I hesitate for a nano-second. I observe the ripple of the inquiry before I reply, as always, "I'm a dancer." A confluence of stuff swims around my head before I utter the truth. I anticipate the next question, "Really? What kind of dance?" and, after a brief statement from me about modern dance, "What's that?" I dread the elaborations that I have to make.

### He Kūnou (A Bow)

My esteemed hula teacher, Kumu Hula Hōkūlani Holt, recently introduced me as a dance educator, which is somewhat correct. I currently direct the 92nd Street Y Harkness Dance Center, which includes the Dance Education Laboratory (DEL), and hold an adjunct position at New York University

Steinhardt School of Culture, Education and Human Resources. I used to run the Education Department at New York City Ballet. For the past few years, I have been supporting and promoting professionals in this discipline of dance education. Although I am a true believer that children of all ages need dance in their educational and cultural lives, the truth is I am still just an *emerging* dance educator. I have much further to go in order to be a *true* dance educator. To be a complete dance educator, in my mind, is to be a dance warrior, like Kumu Hōkū, who does not just teach dance; dance warriors, such as she, preserve the wisdom of an ancient culture and cosmos that was once nearly diminished to extinction. Dance warriors inspire a people, not just a classroom. Rather than dance educator, I prefer to be understood as a perpetual dance student. Whether a developing educator or lifelong learner, I honor and relish the responsibility to help others learn to live as well as live to learn through dance.

## A Spell

Dance has been a quest for meaning and understanding rather than just a matter of doing, a wonderment that frequently drifts beyond knowing and before memory. Like many dancers I know, I dabble in a bit of magical thinking. I make believe. Without knocking the rational powers that the wakeful brain—the dancer's most powerful "muscle"—brings to a dancer's whole being, I also dream. I imagine, which is essential to my awareness of dance things. Certain flights of imagination have been critical for sustaining my ongoing transformation. Dreams of a dance life have morphed into an actual life of dance.

Long before I could walk, talk, and know anything, I danced. I was danced into being through an intimate coupling between my mother and father. Was this conception—an entrance for me that turned a duet into a trio—my first dance? Conceived and en-wombed, I grew and evolved, tumbled and rolled, kicked and prodded, before diving headfirst into a world of the sea-sprayed, rocky shore of Paukūkalo, Maui. And when I eventually walked at 8 months, early for a boy, an ecstatic, brand-new biped was formed. I once precociously fell down a newly discovered landscape, called stairs. Thus, began a series of rises and falls, advancing ebbs and retreating flows, crescendos and decrescendos that texture my dancer's way through the world, a constant rising, spinning, falling, and recovering that would occur again and again.

## A Precipitation

Dad, called A.B.—for Asisclo Baylon, although he preferred to be known by his self-appointed moniker, American Boy—was born in Maglaoi, Ilocos

Norte, Philippines, a muddy village surrounded by rice fields and grazing, gazing—when not hauling—water buffalo. Mom, aka Atang, short for her middle name, Fortunata, was born in Pepeʻekeo, Hawaiʻi, of Visayans from the south-central islands of the Philippine archipelago. He was a northerner; she was a southerner. Although both Filipino, they did not understand each other in their native tongues (Ilocano and Visayan), so they spoke English. They lived during a period of Hawaiian history when the sugar plantations, which ruled the islands' economy and politics, established ethnic camps to separate the immigrant workers and prevent them from forming labor unions. Atang and her family moved to Hamakuapoko, Maui, where they lived uniquely as the only Filipino family in a community designated for Portuguese immigrants. A.B., at age 17, migrated to Maui and ended up in the Puʻunene Filipino camp. A.B. played the violin; Atang the piano. He was a tennis champ; she was a hula dancer. Successful entrepreneurs, they also farmed banana, mango, coconut, taro, watercress, guava, and pomelo. They raised goats and pigs. A.B. and Atang bestowed on their offspring ambition, earthy sensitivity, muscular physicality, a deep respect for community and culture, and a love for music. To assimilate their children and to show them off when guests appeared, my parents required us to learn instrumental music. I started with the piano.

A.B. and Atang also bred dancers. As the fifth of six children, I had older siblings to mold me. They dressed, fed, played with, and scolded me; they took me to the library and read to me; they taught me how to count and tell time; and they showed me how to dance. Although still children themselves, my older sisters were already polished performers of Spanish and Latin American folk dances. Linda, Lolita, and Rosita taught me my first dance form: hula. As a result of their instruction, I staged elaborate solo pageants in our dad's grocery store. An old photo of me displays an ebullient toddler in a diaper and coconut leaf-woven hat, hips mid-*kaʻo* (sway), shaking a pair of *ʻulīʻulī* (feathered gourd rattles) like a professional Waikiki show girl. Strangely, this photo is the only concrete artifact I have of this grand transfiguring part of my life, my first brief moment as a hula dancer.

## A Condemnation

I was a big hit, I am told. Customers commanded performances. Queerly good, probably, for one of the lasting impressions from this period is a distinct burning embarrassment about dance. My swishing hips, graceful arms, and sweet expressions provoked an adverse response from my older brother, Duke, who announced to the world that his baby brother was a "sissy." The rejection stiffened my lovely hula hands and hips. The embarrassment made me a stoic. I became a "boy." Unless one was able to catch one of my solitary, secret dress-up fantasies in my parents' bedroom, the patrons of A.B. Sevilla Store would have to wait another 40 years for my happy hula to resume.

Back then Duke spoke an important, difficult truth to his little brother about dance. Dance can be dangerously subversive in its fleshy honesty and provocative allure. Some people do not get it; some even abhor it. Or they assign and limit it to a gender. Or they find it frivolous entertainment. I suppose it can be difficult to take something seriously when it can and does embody joy, pure and simple. But the dance-phobic appear to suspect and reject deeper, darker, more dangerous pleasures of dance that complicate this notion of superficial frivolity. Dance triggers certain dogmatic religious fears of an uncontrollable, sinful body. We are led to be ashamed of the naughty devil in dance. Because of this strange, fraught interplay of grace, fun, fear, and flesh, we, dancers and non-dancers alike, are not always *comfortable* in our bodies. I have spent a life exploring and masking this profound discomfort.

For me, the stunting of a toddler male hula dancer is archetypical of grander cultural fears and historical misperceptions about hula and dance that started in the early 1800s, when evangelical Calvinist missionaries arrived in the islands and declared the native dance lewd and lascivious. Hula, like me, went underground. A century-and-a-half later, dance teacher-warriors, like Kumu Hōkū and her hula educators, rescued a cultural practice and, as a consequence, a whole culture. Yet Duke—the eventual high school football all-star, Marine Corp grunt, and head lifeguard on the island—would come around to appreciate the kinesthetic vocations, from sport to dance. In fact, one of his sons would become, after going to college on a football scholarship, a professional Polynesian dancer at a lū'au production. Such karmic resolutions give me comfort in the potential of dance to sway and enlighten the non-dancing other.


## A Reincarnation


An untraceable proto-memory of dance, a primordial dream, spins further back than my Maui conception and childhood. For me, dance is a talk with the dead, a way to communicate with and mediate the ancestors. Dance resurrects legacy. As much as my Republican parents instituted deep respect for their adopted secure, free, and brave American homeland, they encouraged a fierce pride in their Filipino-ness. We were baptized Roman Catholics, but A.B. instigated a personal Reformation. The St. Anthony Catholic School nuns wanted to keep Duke back a grade. He was a small, hyperactive, distracted kid, who could not sit still to learn. A.B. protested, and the entire Sevilla family immediately became products of the public school system.

We joined an Episcopalian congregation composed entirely of Filipinos, which suited A.B. just fine because the whole service was spoken in his percussive Ilocano tongue.

When I turned 10 years old, our adopted church's youth choir had a makeover. The older boys were entering puberty; their angelic voices were deepening. The wife of the reverend, Manang (older sister) Nancy Andres, who also was the choir mistress, then reorganized us as a troupe of Filipino folk dancers. The transformation began as a way for the congregation to participate with other Filipino community organizations in a huge annual event on the island that celebrated Philippine culture, called the Barrio Fiesta. During the fiesta, groups erected traditional *nipa* (grass) huts, demonstrated cultural traditions, cooked and sold Filipino delicacies, and engaged in numerous athletic and artistic competitions. The biggest prize was the folk dance competition, which Manang Nancy had determined we would win. Hence, from the hula ashes of shame arose a phoenix of a Filipino folk dancer.

We were transformed into a troupe of disciplined dancing youth and soundly beat the older competition. But rather than liturgical dancers of a church, we became poster children of Philippine culture throughout the islands. The dancing Good Shepherd Church Filipino Youth Choir eventually toured the West Coast, from British Columbia to Los Angeles. We even performed at Disneyland. And although much of what I embodied was theatricized folkloric choreography of traditional rituals and practices, I nonetheless developed a burning fascination for this and ultimately *any* culture's dance forms.

Back then, my parents encouraged me to dance. They firmly and incorrectly promoted the stereotype that Filipinos are *by nature* good dancers, if not *the best* dancers in the world. Sure, notions of "good" and "best" are subjective and culture-bound, but if any truth can be told of Filipinos, we come from a demonstrative country of dance. The YouTube phenomenon of hundreds of orange jumpsuit-clad, proud Filipino prisoners performing their elaborate rendition of Michael Jackson's *Thriller* (1983) and other staged movement choirs to American and Filipino pop songs is illustrative of this kinesthetic nation. I was a Philippine folk dancer and absorbed the canon of this dance tradition.

As a choir member and then later, I learned ceremonies of courtship, harvest, battle, and death. I reenacted social cariñosas for celebration as well as ceremonies to ward off evil spirits. I performed the bombastic trance dances of the indigenous tribes of the northern mountains and the serpentine Muslim choreography of the southern islands. We restaged colonial reinterpretations of continental standards (jotas, mazurkas, paso dobles, waltzes, fandangos, polkas, etc.). We stomped under a full moon. We prayed for rain. We mimicked birds and fish. As we stepped and leaped and spun, we banged on gongs and struck sticks, castanets, bamboo poles and coconut shells. We sang courtship songs and drinking songs. We danced on wooden benches. We wielded fans, swords, shields, kerchiefs, and blankets; we balanced wine glasses and candles and clay pots on our heads. We breathed into history as it breathed ancient lives into us.

## A Stumble

Despite such ethnic pride and the renown of the Good Shepherd Youth Choir, the onset of puberty generated enough panic for me to run away from dance. At only 14 years of age, without any bullying, name-calling other, I was suddenly anxious of being seen dancing and being challenged on my masculinity. I quit the choir and retreated—another rise and fall— to my dance closet, secretly dreaming of an opportunity to do what was so organically fulfilling yet seemed so unwelcome. Other than H. Wayne Mendoza, a Philippine folk dance professor at the University of Hawai'i at Mānoa who came to Maui to teach us new dances, I had too few male role models or mentors to guide me. Strong masculine cultural images of José Limón, Paul Taylor, Rudolf Nureyev, and Mikhail Baryshnikov had yet to appear on my horizon. The popular Fred Astaire and Gene Kelly seemed effete in my pubescent context. Hip hop and MTV had barely been born to highlight cool guys dancing. Furthermore, the Stonewall Revolution and the contemporary attitudes about gender and sexual orientation—complicated inchoate sensations that commingled with my shame about dance—had yet to gain traction politically or personally in my provincial, confused, adolescent sphere. No wonder I still hesitate when asked what I do. Vestiges of those early dance experiences remain with me, and I acknowledge this miasma of recollections in each personal declaration of who I am.

## A Rebound

As an English major at the UH Mānoa, I mustered enough bravery to join a Filipino folk dance troupe, Pamana Dancers, in which my sister Rosita had been performing. The director and mentor, Hana Gomez Trinidad, sent me to the Philippines one summer to study with the Bayanihan, the national folkloric dance company that trained her. When I returned to Hawai'i, I was expected to teach the dances I had only just learned. A rehearsal had been arranged at a studio with a catchy name, Dances We Dance. The school— located above a venerable Chinese restaurant from which thick aromas of the stir-fried and the steamed constantly wafted—was run by a couple, Betty Jones and Fritz Ludin, who had relocated from New York City.

I arrived at the Pamana practice early and found a bench to wait for the rest of the troupe. While waiting, I found myself observing something strange: another dance rehearsal. In the piece, a man and two women, charged through space, linking arms, breaking apart, reconnecting, and attacking the air with unusually exuberant arcing, leaping, and propelling movements. The sweep of purposeful abandonment silenced me. Although I lacked the words then to articulate the stuff that jolted me, I somatically understood something deep, idiosyncratic, and moving. The dance was *Invention* by Doris Humphrey, choreographed in 1948, a nearly forgotten work that the company restaged and notated for posterity.

Fortunately, Betty and Fritz, recognizing my awe, asked me if I wanted to study this thing called Modern Dance. Thus began my initiation into "concert dance" and the Humphrey-Weidman-Limón principles, which were developed in the nascent stages of Modern Dance. I soon found myself in a daily ritual of reaching, curving, rising, falling, rebounding, breathing, sweating, traveling, discovering, and dancing. Betty was the original Desdemona in Limón's *The Moor's Pavanne* (1949) and her husband, Fritz, also danced in the Limón Dance Company. They became my mentors. Few dancers are as evolved embodiments of that philosophical and organic approach of the Humphrey-Weidman-Limón technique—whereby motion is generated by the planet's gravitational attraction and humanity's kinesthetic and aesthetic acknowledgment—than Betty, who is for me another mighty dance warrior. She teaches to this day with unwavering, motivational focus. At their studio, among a community of people who worshipped at the altar of dance, I found a practice for life. I learned how to rebound from a fall.

## An Arrival

Against my parents' wishes, I chose the dance vocation. I was on the down low because, although my parents loved and promoted learning in the arts, heaven forbid one of their own would opt for dance as a profession! A.B. and Atang wanted me—their ambitious and always-wanting-to-be-loved student who achieved all of those superior marks and glowing distinctions (trophies, medals, certificates, citations, newspaper articles!)—to go to law or medical school. Ostensibly, I had promise in other fields besides dance. Imagine the disappointed shock and awe when I announced my decision, after graduating with highest honors, to move to New York City to become a dancer with only $500 to my name. For this anguished decision, I have to honor the late Jack Unterecker, the poet, biographer, professor, and dance writer at UH Mānoa, who responded to my dilemma by saying, "What's wrong with wanting to make beauty?"

I had given myself 2 years to achieve the goal of making beauty. I had not come to the acknowledgment that I had already been dancing beautiful things my whole life. To me, and perhaps this narrow perception was a legitimization determined by the greater culture, becoming a *real* dancer meant getting a full-time job in dance. In other words, *working* in dance rather than *living* in dance, two distinct ideas that are not separate, just nuanced. Toward this goal, I set myself on a disciplined regimen of class, rehearsal, and work bussing tables and hosting at the Grand Hyatt Hotel, with rushed moments to grab a sandwich or take-out. I suffered through the performing artist-gypsy period that most young dancers experience once they have moved to New York City. I took every possible dance gig (often unpaid) that I could squeeze out of my body. But, nearing the end of the second year, I found myself still in search of a job and legitimacy.

## A Slip; A Catch; A Pratfall

"What are you reading?" asked Robby Barnett, artistic director of Pilobolus, as he drove me to the train station after one of my callbacks. We then pursued a long conversation about Wallace Stevens, the poet laureate of Connecticut, where the company also resided. Was this chat part of my audition? I wondered. Nevertheless, I knew from that moment onward that this company required, more than just physical skills, learnedness from its dancers. And there was something else: luck. Being in the right place at the right time. Serendipity. Kismet. Perhaps gratitude makes one think of dance "success" as a result of such uncontrollable happy accidents. For how many dance organizations can actually support a company of dancers? Too few, so I cannot help feeling deeply appreciative that the stars were aligned and I was hired just as I was beginning to plan a return to Hawai'i.

So-called success, however, takes more than a belief in fatalistic, magical thinking. A dance life requires resilience and courage to manifest energetic motion because risks will be taken, hopefully responsible ones, and challenges and disappointments are unavoidable. I had experienced too many times the beautiful fate of falling that resulted always in the rise of another stage in a dance life. The will of a dancer must be firm and pliant. Most importantly, to seize the few and fleeting opportunities, I concur with the sages that dance requires education, the essential *plié* before the literal and metaphoric leap.

Oddly, I had never seen Pilobolus, one of the major inventors of modern dance genius during our time. I was an innocent to the company as much as the company was an innocent to the dance world. The troupe appeared in the early 1970s, when four brainy jocks from Dartmouth, under the tutelage of Alison Chase, began to perform these wildly witty, unconventional, athletic, and evocative dances that caused audiences to ask: "Is this dance?" My previous training in dance, however, came from the established, respectable generation of (capital "M") Modern (capital "D") Dance. Pilobolus, named after the feisty phototropic fungus that Jonathan Wolken, an original member, researched in his father's biophysics lab, didn't seem to care about those capital letters. The company was not interested in the dance legacies of Isadora Duncan or Ruth St. Denis, despite sharing the same pioneering spirit of counterculture iconoclasm. They just wanted to create original, thrilling movement from their vast collective imagination and intellect. Unlike the serious and precious art I had studied previously, Pilobolus loved to goof and make fun.

I naïvely only knew that I wanted this gig. Actually, the lingering rumor about the company being homophobic did concern me, but the talk proved to be false. Pilobolus back then, despite all the erotic male partnering—an unaffected innovation and remarkable contribution to concert dance—was unusually straight, homosocial but not homophobic. As far as I know, I was only the second dancer in the company's history who was out of the closet. The male-on-male dance seemed an expression of irreverence and liberty. The original dancers, who later became the artistic directors, explained that they clung to each other because they did not know how to dance alone. They discovered safety and ingenuity in the signature connections, counterbalances, entwinements of partnering that eventually became emblematic of their collaborative process.

Despite the eventual popularity and accessibility of the art, Pilobolus had never firmly and wholeheartedly identified itself as part of the modern dance community. Based in the bucolic, rolling hills of Litchfield County, the "Pils" rather enjoyed their non-New York City, outsider-art status. Although the company sold out its New York City run, the critics seemed ambivalent about its accessibility and choreography-by-committee process. When I joined, Pilobolus was entirely Caucasian. If Asian Americans may own such claims, I may have broke the color barrier. I thus perceived myself as an outsider among outsiders; however, the company embraced me, and Pilobolus became my new family name. We were only six back then, four men and two women, a neat contrast to my real family of four women and two men. We traveled throughout the world most often by ourselves and with a small crew of production specialists.

Still, I needed some time to settle into this dance community that was predominantly male and macho. In my experience, dance had been the province of women, strong women; my dance community had been saturated with women. In Pilobolus, I found myself in the company of apparently straight alpha males. The first dance I collaborated on was *Particle Zoo* (1990). The choreographic process involved just seven men—four dancers and three artistic directors. The collective testosterone in the ensuing rehearsals generated a dizzying competitive one-up-man-ship that constantly compelled each dancer and director to out-perform the other. A genius of Pilobolus is the tacit understanding that any imaginative idea is choreographically explorable, if not performable, in every mutable way. We were dared and inspired to flaunt our physical skill and creative flair, and were pushed with what seemed like impossible propositions. After day 1 of this work, I was zapped emotionally and crippled physically. I could not lower my body into the bathtub; I could not do stairs. What had I fallen into this time? Back then, the company had a smirky diagnosis for this inevitable, excruciating condition of paralysis—"polio." My body recovered, and my first dance with Pilobolus, a composition about particle physics, became a relentless, propulsive romp of competitive, collaborative masculine fight and flight.

I admit, the Pilobolus job provided the career credibility and affirmation that dancers seek. But after 7 years, I knew I could not sustain this physical and creative rigor any longer. I realized, sadly, that a job in Pilobolus—most awesome as the experience was—could not be my whole life. I had to move on, travel less, yet experience more. I thought teaching was next, so I went to graduate school at Teachers College, Columbia University and the University of Wisconsin-Milwaukee, where I continued to investigate my ongoing quest on how to sustain a holistic life of embodying, reflecting, cultivating, and dreaming dance.

## A Genuflection

When I was in high school, a group of classmates and I enrolled in the chemistry honors class. Mr. Omuro, a quiet and compact figure with deep fissures of wrinkles on his brow and a severely buzzed flat top, taught the class. He rode his bike to school every day. The class was a college preparatory course, made up of the allegedly smart students. After a few weeks of poor performances in lab assignments and quizzes, however, Mr. Omuro announced that he was going to teach us something "more important than chemistry." He said that we could not mention any of this to our parents, administrators, or teachers, which intrigued us in ways that any investigation of the periodic table could not. So every Friday, we gathered in his storage closet and sat cross-legged in a circle. A massage therapist for the school's athletic teams, he showed us how to roll on tennis balls to treat strained muscles. He discussed aspects of the more metaphysical sciences. We meditated. He told us how the first and last thought of each day should be gratefulness for having had this day, for awaking, for living. He, this chemistry teacher, showed us how to hold our hands together when we prayed. "The fingers must point toward heaven so the prayer gets directed there."

Mr. Omuro had suffered a heart attack a few years earlier. To manage his condition, he had turned his stressful life toward the cultivation of something that to this day I constantly try to identify and integrate. What is more important than chemistry? What transcends all knowledge of the structures and behaviors of our physical world? If this wisdom was so potent, why keep such teachings separate and silent from the rest of the school? Why did the inner sanctum of this secret, significant exploration have to take place in another closet? What was this sacred intelligence that could not be shared? Sitting in reflection? Healing? Being thankful? Can one accomplish such important things through dance?

## A Harvest

Preparation determines who and what I am. The Hawaiian word for such readiness is *ho'omākaukau*, a key tenet in hula. The *kumu hula* (teacher) asks before each dance, "*Ho'omākaukau?*" Are you prepared? The *haumāna* (students) reply, " *'Ae.*" Yes, we are ready. How else, but through education, does one know where the feet and the ground must meet to stand tall, bend low, step, or spin? How do we appreciate the beautiful significance of any fortuitous recovery and daring discovery? How else, but through preparation and reflection, do we find meaning in any experience?

Dance has evolved into more than just *doing* for me. This perspective may explain the pause that precedes my response to the question, "What do you do?" I dance, but I also am, existentially, a dancer. I moreover redefine and conflate the nonexclusive states of doing and being dance into the one complex continuum of *becoming*, an ongoing conversation and investigation of what was, is and can be. Because the world is huge, the people are many, and life is short, I became a nomad, a wayfaring journeyman in search of the tubular wave of a dance experience and, as I tried to vanquish queer dance demons of a past, a meaning of manhood. I had not acknowledged that I already stood stage center of a real dance experience, alive to a moment, alert to humanity, attuned to the inevitability of change. A peripatetic, I ascribed to the delicious rise and fall, curving through and around memory and modernity, merging personal, cultural and cosmological spheres. All along the way, folks from my history have been speaking to me—teasing, nagging, and instructing me—incessantly. I am trying to listen. I am becoming more attentive to this work-in-progress, called a life. I am becoming a dancer, a lifer, a lifelong learner, and an emerging educator.

What do I do? I am dancing. I am harnessing the courage to become a warrior. With ancient roots, I am becoming cellularly, organically, centrifugally, centripetally a ninja dancer, swooping through the past and potential to be present, transfiguring, sweating, dealing, healing, heaving, moving gravity, breathing gratitude, now, magically, soul planted, fingers pointed to heaven, whirling, spiraling . . . here and there.

*Dedicated To Becky Jung (1965–2011), a lifer.*

# 7

## Pieces of the Past
## Swim into the Present

### Linda Caldwell

A story is like a dance. It takes at least two people to make it come to life, the one who does the telling and the one who does the listening. Sometimes the roles are reversed, and the giver becomes the taker. We both do the talking, we both listen, and even the silences become loaded. From a small number of perfectly ordinary words a tapestry takes shape, suggestive of a dream, but close enough to a reality that, more often than not, remains elusive. It is a feat of mutual trust, of mutual imagining. What matters is whether or not we can believe each other's voices, and the test of that will lie in the story we make together. It will lie in the pieces of the past that swim into the present.

—Joydeep Roy-Bhattacharya (*The Storyteller of Marrakesh*)

### Float and Paddle

As my own past at times elegantly floats and, at many other times, furiously dog paddles into the present, I continue to discover clear voices speaking and coaxing me along the way. These voices weave their own stories and, as I learn to listen to their cadences, I remember backwards and think the following dance story forward.

## Pieces of the Past

I was an 8-year-old girl living in 1950s Melbourne, Florida, a small town rapidly being developed by the multiply constructed, suburban tract homes built for the burgeoning families of World War II veterans. My parents had just allowed me the freedom to walk alone to my friend's house two streets away—a momentous landmark in life to that point. The night before my anticipated visit, I had a dream, one I have never forgotten. In my dream memory, I find myself beginning a long, solo journey through my neighborhood. As I walk, I wave at people working in their newly sodded yards as others wash the Florida ocean salt off their cars. I play with the neighbors' dogs gamboling beside me. I remember the feel of walking, the wonderful physicality of freedom as each new step, each new sight, opened possibilities for the directions my journey might take. With each choice of dream path taken, I find myself repeating out loud, over and over again, "Oh, how I wish I had a pencil, then I would be able to write down and remember forever all the wonderful things happening even as they disappear in front of me." As I continue my dream-walking through disappearing terrains in which color and shapes shift around me, the sun begins to set. I come unexpectedly upon a motel and decide to stay the night. We had recently returned from a family vacation up the Eastern seaboard and my father showed me how to register at each of the many small and, often times, whacky motels appearing along U.S. Route 1. In my dream, I walk up to the motel's sign-in desk, climb up a conveniently placed stool, and peer down at the large registration book. After reading the names and wanting so much to add my own name to the list, I ring the bell calling the attendant from a back room. He advances, turns to me, smiles, and slowly queries: "Do you need a pencil?"

Today, I write my story on a laptop computer with the print and uniformity of the text seemingly more permanent than those resulting from the often fragile and quickly diminishing lead of my childhood pencil. However, similar to my childhood dream, my journey moves improvisationally with voices calling me to discover memories as "pieces of the past that swim into the present" (2011, p. 5).

## Lucy in the Sky

In 1966, I entered Melbourne High School with Dr. B. Frank Brown as principal. Dr. Brown arrived with the mission to create a "cutting-edge" educational atmosphere—a high-achieving environment that would attract engineers and their families to Florida, then considered something of a swampy backwater, as they joined the developing NASA missile program at Cape Canaveral. Dr.

Brown brought in disciplines of study previously unheard of in our sleepy southern town. Within 1 year, he had developed experimental grading systems and set up curricula in which we could explore Russian history, art and architecture, and, something quite unknown to us at that time, modern dance. Prior to this remarkable change, most of my friends' and my experiences of dance developed as we dreamily and frenetically performed to Motown hits and the Beatles' tunes or, as children, we sat mesmerized in front of the television watching the June Taylor dancers' bodies create kaleidoscopic geometries on the hugely popular *Jackie Gleason Show*.

My sense of dance changed dramatically after enrolling in my first modern dance class in high school and being introduced to our teacher, Donald Steele. Mr. Steele had graduated with a master's in modern dance from the University of Utah, a course of study I could not imagine at the time. He opened up and brought to life the world of art for me; he took art out of the museum living in my mind, and made art actively move inside my body. Mr. Steele taught us to "know" movement: to knowingly feel how dance communicated through our bodies. My first solo was created that year to the Beatles' "Lucy in the Sky with Diamonds." Not only was I able to picture myself sailing "in a boat on a river, with tangerine trees and marmalade skies," I could also feel myself moving with that boat and through those trees while gazing at the sky. I fell in love with the physicality of that feeling.

## Ricocheting Change

In 1974, after spending a tumultuous 5 years in three different colleges switching majors many times, I landed at the University of Iowa where I decided to continue my original high school plan to become an English teacher. I could not yet conceive of dance as a career option and my parents certainly did not see a life in dance as anything they could actively support. During my last year at the university, I noticed that courses in modern dance, as well as in golf, bowling, and archery, were being offered and that they fulfilled my needed requirements in "leisure studies." Deciding to enter the world of modern dance again, I learned about movement from dancer, choreographer, and musician Marcia Claire Belsher Thayer. During one class, Professor Thayer was absent and the student assistant rolled in a 16-mm projector so we could watch a filmed version of Anna Sokolow's 1955 choreography, *Rooms*. After many sputtering stops and starts and the constant fear of the film breaking, we finally saw the dance. In this viewing, I felt movement telling a story in which real people lived, not in a fairy tale, but within a hauntingly solitary space of one chair, with many lone chairs creating a staged community of rooms. Enlivened emotions pulsed through the entire body of each dancer extending and connecting each danced room to the viewing room in which I sat. Sokolow brought to life imaginary spaces in a manner that I had not experienced in my previous creative writing classes. I walked out of the room knowing the pre-imagined picture of my future was altered, even though no clear image came into view to replace the original design. Later that semester, when consulting the library's new subscription of *Dance Magazine*, I saw an advertisement for a receptionist at the Dance Notation Bureau (DNB) in New York City. I rushed off an application that was accepted—mostly due to my recently acquired typing skills—and found myself working with Maria Grandy and Muriel (Mickey) Topaz, as well as many other emerging notators who continually passed through the DNB office at 19 Union Square West.

## Pieces of the Past

Union Square, New York City: a major subway center and a space for farmer's markets, war protests, and drug sales in the night hours. I get off the No. 1 subway train, weave through the underground tunnels, and surface to the excitement of a New York City morning. I enter a tall, narrow building and step into an ancient elevator that fits only two people. Pushing the up button, I slowly and creakily rise. The door opens onto the small, informal lobby of the DNB. The odor of cinnamon muffins, brought in daily by Anne the accountant, lures me to my corner desk. Jane Marriott, a budding notator, greets me as her dog Butter makes quick work of a muffin. I put my homework face down on my desk trying to hide the symbols crazily placed all over the page. As part of my job, I was learning how to type Labanotation with the new IBM Selectric typewriter ball, a skill for which I had little talent. I wander down the hall to replace dance notation scores in the DNB library and pass Irmgard Bartenieff's office, where she is already deeply engrossed in work. The DNB represents a creation of love by a group of amazing, dedicated women.

After moving into the Evangeline, a temporary Greenwich Village home for young women, I began my work as a DNB employee in charge of organizing studio rentals for choreographers needing rehearsal space. One such choreographer was Anna Sokolow herself. Surreptitiously, I would sneak peeks at her rehearsals on the pretense of filing library materials in the next room until asked by Ms. Sokolow, in no uncertain terms, to desist. Later, the DNB gave me the opportunity to study Labanotation for free even though I was neither particularly interested nor particularly good at the practice. In the process of learning Labanotation, an amazing discovery emerged for me—the success of the notational system and its practice depended on creating consistent relationships between the principles underlying the practice. If I changed one principle other related principles had to shift in order to keep the system's intent and purpose clear. In fact, the need to make changes, which ricocheted throughout the entire system, kept the practitioners engaged and committed to future developments as the needs of the dance field changed over time. This example of how one adapts to change—whether change in ideas, practice, or spatial relationships within new environments—in order to move forward and remain engaged has stayed with me over the ensuing years. The staff at the DNB showed how to take on the challenge of documenting an ever-changing dance world while also making that challenge exciting and energizing.

## Leading With My Tail

While working at the DNB, I discovered the studios of Alwin Nikolais where one could go on a Saturday for 3 hours to take dance technique and impro- visation/choreography. Here I could listen and play with the movement ideas of Phyllis Lamhut as she guided beginning dancers to move with, not just in, space. I never knew dance was something I could shape with space in the moment of moving.

### Pieces of the Past

I am in the middle of the line of beginning dancers. I look at the slight woman sitting behind the big, sonorous drums inviting us to move. She yells, "Lead with your tail!" The dancer in front of me spirals around as her tail calls me to travel in space with her. My tail spins; I am astonished as my ears and my eyes move through my tail. My tail calls to other tails as they follow me, as I follow them, as our energies lead us together. We are "graining" and . . . whoops . . . I become self-conscious, the moment of being in the movement disappears. I close my eyes and let my tail listen; I feel myself being drawn through space. Oh how I wish I had a pencil at this moment to write what I feel.

Like the DNB, the Nikolais classes created another world in which systems of "knowing and practice," knowing in the body principles of motion even as they change in the moment of practice, were supported by the dancer's commitment to discover constantly new ways for the body to move through and with time and space. The sense of commitment as a precursor to success was certainly not new to me, but the idea of commitment to an idea, to a way of working, to a way of learning and living in the world, was not something I had fully realized to this point. I began to understand that commitment was not about loudly pushing my ideas into the world with a bellicose voice. Rather, such dedication was about listening with the entire body, about softening the body in order to hear through the muscles and bones. Even more, listening required an openness to following, a skill developed in the moment of doing. Throughout the rest of my life's journey, I found that this skill of listening/following was not an easy act to accomplish.

I began to question how I might find a way to record how actively listening felt. I learned how to record movement in Labanotation. But how could I write about committing to being in the moment of moving? Nikolais's ideas and Phyllis Lamhut's teaching opened this question in my life. I also realized at this point in my ongoing journey that there was much more to this thing called dance than I had ever imagined. Developing skills to bring these newly emerging moments of felt movement alive and then developing a way to communicate these lively moments to others was something I wanted so much to achieve. I was, however, still waiting for someone to hand me that metaphorical pencil with which I could share my sense of dance with an audience.

## The Intricate Delicacy

While walking with a friend to the Nikolais studios in downtown Manhattan and watching the towers of the World Trade Center rise to redefine the skyline of New York and the image of America's power, we discussed at length dance as the performance of abstract aesthetics in contrast to dance as a moving representation of real-life or human experience. These discussions provoked us to participate in a workshop conducted by mime Stefan Niedzialkowski who was at that time a member of Henrik Tomaszewski's Wrocław Pantomime Theater. At that time, Poland was tightly hidden behind the Iron Curtain, a country practically unknown to us. Expecting to learn certain tricks like how to create a pretend wall or catch invisible fluttering butterflies, I was surprised to find Niedzialkowski presenting the mime artist as a physical magician who creates illusory fantasies performed through principles of muscular resistance while, simultaneously, developing "readable" images of the viewer's every day, lived reality. In other words, the mime could provide viewers with a way to feel the energy within the seemingly inert objects around them, making the world alive and vibrant in new ways.

### Pieces of the Past

Niedzialkowski sits alone in a spotlight combing his imaginary long tresses. He becomes a woman before my eyes. The immense sense of enlivened joy passing through his body as his fingers feel the intricate delicacy of the flowing hair makes me shiver. I watch his body feel the air as the hair lifts away from his shoulders then sense the weight of the hair cascading down his back. Suddenly, he pulls out a pair of make believe scissors and, in one brisk moment, snips the hair at its roots. In this moment, he acknowledges the audience for the first time, looking at us one by one. Slowly, he offers the cut hair to us with a smile. Then, as a beautifully poised woman, he exits the stage.

After watching Niedzialkowski's magically shifting images, I realized that, once again, an artist was asking me to look deeply at the possibilities for how my future practice might take shape. Over the years, I have interpreted this story in many ways depending on my outlook on life at the time. However, what has not changed for me is Niedzialkowski's ability to bring to life the abstract beauty of that "felt" moment while creating an image of a real person moving within the sinew and nerve endings of my own body. In this way, Niedzielkowski added an element of trickery to his artistic request. He invited me to disappear as performer so that the viewers could find their own imaginative scenarios in the staged moment of performance. Paradoxically, the act of disappearing within the performance is not a passive act; rather, the performer is deeply present as she creates imaged possibilities through the resistance and release of her muscles in space. In this space, terrains of viewings are brought to life for the audience. The extent of what Niedzialkowski was asking me to understand did not become fully transparent until much later in my life when studying to be a dance researcher and writer. As a researcher, I am now also being asked to continually develop methods for foregrounding the voices of the research participants while actively moving my voice to the background. Within the moving and repositioning of these disparate voices, I find spaces are opened for diverse readings of the research.

## Haunting Questions

While in New York, each new experience, each new lesson learned, shifted my own understanding of modern, or what was becoming termed *contemporary postmodern*, dance. This new dance seemed to be based in the paradoxical practice of a movement discipline in which one attempted to appear random and pedestrian, caught in the moment and improvisational. Complicating this disparity between formal technique and the need to say "NO" to technique was how this dance practice could also connect to and bring to life the very real problems surrounding American culture in the 1970s. As the Vietnam War became more heated and deeply controversial, I felt torn between values developed while being brought up as a 1950s "army brat" and values being shaped by my new life as a college graduate studying contemporary dance, an artistic practice that often seemed intellectually distant from the disturbing images evoked on nightly television of the killing fields in Southeast Asia. While receiving letters from my mother about hometown friends coming back to America from Vietnam in body bags, I was dancing. Trying to discover how dance could portray the emotions, the desires, the needs, of an America lost in conflict was something I knew must be pursued. Video images of war, of preponderant space races, and emotional newscasts of idealistic people being assassinated also became the impetus for the dancers and dance writers around me. These two groups grappled with how contemporary dance could be meaningful beyond intellectual, aesthetic discourse. Questions concerning purpose, meaning, and the ethics of an artist's life swirled around me, animating conversations found within the crossroads of a 1970s New York City.

I wondered, how could Nikolais's sense of moment-to-moment commitment to the performance of time, space, shape, and energy help solve the huge social problems facing American society? Can my love of dance move beyond my own moment-to-moment enjoyment in order to spark responsible action towards the world around me? How might my personal love affair with dance become something that moves beyond my own needs? These questions haunted me as I strove to not only experience joy while moving in space, but to also develop the awareness that, until all bodies have the freedom to feel this joy, our moving bodies can at any moment be suppressed. This awareness of suppression took on more poignancy after finding myself, 10 years later, working with Polish and Polish Jewish dance artists who sustained their identities through their dancing bodies over many centuries of censorship.

## Pieces of the Past

University of Iowa, Iowa City, in the early 1970s: The Grand Union dance theater improvisational group performs on campus. Many universities on the Interstate 90 highway from Boston to Seattle were accustomed to touring groups appearing unexpectedly on their campuses. The Grand Union performance takes place as the Vietnam War draft lottery broadcasts over the radio. Young men listen to the radio as an announcer pulls birth dates randomly from a pool. The earlier your birthday is called, the sooner you board a flight to fight. I hear sobs as 19-year-olds listen to their fates being announced. While watching the Grand Union dig deeply into this politically charged turmoil through moment-to-moment improvisation, I sense performance as a space in which provocative issues can be brought to life right in front of the audience. Together, as a community, we can experience our group fears, joys, and challenges, sharing our cultural stories from numerous insights with moments of learning, listening, and loving.

## The Alarm Clock Rings

After 3 years of working and playing in New York, I had depleted my savings. I had to make a decision: either I stay in New York and look for paid work or use the little savings I had left to underwrite a new dance journey. By this time, I knew dance was in my life to stay. After years of living "in the now," I realized that the future did exist and that I would need to support myself. I asked myself: When my alarm goes off in the morning, what kind of day do I want? How do I set goals to make that kind of day happen? Looking for possible answers to these questions, a friend and I went to the New York Public Library, retrieved university catalogues, and began to search for graduate programs (Google did not yet exist) where I could enter as a novice dancer and my friend could study international trade unions, a hot topic in the middle of the 1970s. Together, we settled on the University of Wisconsin-Madison where dance as an academic pursuit was first established through the teaching and writings of Margaret H'Doubler. After working full time for a year to gain Wisconsin residency so I could pay in-state tuition, I registered as a 28-year-old master of fine arts (MFA) student and began the study of dance within this academic setting. To my chagrin, I was given a graduate assistantship teaching ballroom and folk dance classes, two dance forms in which I was a complete novice. However, no matter how sophisticated my practice in contemporary or modern dance became over time, ballroom and folk dance, as well as my experience in Labanotation, were what actually allowed me to enter, if only through the back door, the world of dance in higher education.

## Opening Landscapes

My first teaching job after graduating with an MFA was at the University of Wisconsin-Stevens Point (UWSP) and came about at the last moment when the candidate of choice accepted another position elsewhere. My first teaching duties included ballroom, square, and folk dance, plus beginning ballet, Labanotation, and multiple levels of modern dance. I also was expected to choreograph for the department musicals, something I had never before attempted. Surprisingly, however, while stumbling through my attempts to teach these new techniques and styles in a manner that would engage my students, I discovered myself becoming wonderfully lost in the unfamiliar movement territory opening before me. Within these moments of disorientation, more ideas, more practices, more ways of discussing what is dance emerged. As my dance landscape opened, I found musicians, visual artists, and theater practitioners, both professionals and students, also wandering throughout my newly discovered territory. In my drifting, I tripped on the act of collaboration, an act in which the art of connecting diverse ideas and practices developed as discoveries emerged from those connections.

## Shared Bicycles

My first collaborative activity took place as the choreographer and music score reader for the 1980 musical, *Tintypes*. To learn what principles guided choreography for musicals, I had the privilege of observing UWSP faculty member Jim Moore, former company member and rehearsal director with Jerome Robbins. Jim taught me how to energize empty spaces while bringing the music, the text, and the narrative plots to life. Through him, and my need to create an exciting production of *Tintypes*, I found myself learning how to create music collages with musician Steven Senski and art collages with visual artist Carol Emmons. I discovered how the dance and theater students performing in the musical brought diverse talents to rehearsals, making each an unpredictable place for learning. Worlds and paths within these worlds opened up exponentially. With each new collaboration, I was given gifts for how to create, discuss, and write about where dance might go in tandem with other artists; we were all pedaling together on our dance, theater, art, and music bicycles built for two, three, four, and more.

While learning to find balance on these newly acquired and shared bicycles, I realized that distinctions and limitations made between disciplines, especially between theatre and dance, were holding my imagination at bay. The seed for desiring to sense dance as connected to other disciplines had been sown, if not yet realized, in an elective theatre history course taught by Dr. Esther Jackson during my graduate studies. Dr. Jackson's life as one of the first African American doctoral students in theater drew me to her class; I wondered what kept her energized and in love with a discipline no matter how difficult the pursuit of a career was for her at that time in America. Through Dr. Jackson's lectures, the study of theater and dance was presented as the motor, the electricity, powering an emerging American culture in the 20th century. In her very formal classroom we were called on, always by our proper names (Ms. Caldwell), to verbally articulate how the materials delivered in class might further our personal practice of theater or dance. Dr. Jackson then actively probed our insights. I felt her passion in every moment of that questioning as she opened layers of language in which historical stories moved over time and into the present. To this day, I have all of the notes I took while in Dr. Jackson's class. Now, I look back and wonder if my own passion for learning about dance as theatre and theater as dance can enliven the notes of my own students.

## Unpredictable Landscapes

The connections developed between theater and dance during graduate school created an exciting bond with fellow theater students, one of whom was Allen Kuharski. Allen later became a Fulbright scholar studying theater arts in Poland, which was and still is a forerunner in innovative scene design and graphic layout for theatrical posters. In the mid-1980s, Allen introduced my choreographic work to performance artist Joseph Chaikin (1935-2003) who was then working in San Francisco. In 1959, Joe joined the Living Theatre, a 1950s-1960s New York experimental group of theater and movement artists directed by Judith Malina and Julian Beck. In 1963, Joe founded the Open Theater, an avant-garde experimental ensemble performance group in which he continued to explore how to create and direct exciting collaborative theater works. Joe also assisted Peter Brook in various Royal Shakespeare productions, mounted a production of *The Dybbuk* (1914) in Israel, and conducted workshops with experimental theater director Jerzy Grotowski in Poland. In 1984, Joe suffered a stroke leaving him aphasic. I met him 3 years after his stroke and began working with him in San Francisco as a choreographer and movement coach for two of his evolving performances.

While working with Joe, I once again found myself listening very closely to ideas emerging in the process of rehearsal while translating these ideas into movement for the actors. Joe brought writers, actors, and musicians together into each rehearsal where he would then introduce differing plot scenarios that could be "played with" through text and movement as the writers and musicians developed scripts and scores emerging from the improvisations. In this setting, I learned how to "trust the process," a phrase I heard repeated over the years, but one I had difficulty understanding in practice; letting go of artistic control seemed somewhat nonintuitive to me. After time, I realized that trusting the process did not mean letting go but instead meant paying close attention, watching with a keen eye, and developing a pinpoint ability to concentrate on each moment of action. Through this rigorous process, movement theater emerged in ways the choreographer or director could not predict.

Learning how to navigate through unpredictable landscapes was a gift offered by Joe Chaikin, but was not the only one he generously shared. He also introduced me to the work of Jerzy Grotowski whose 1968 text, *Towards a Poor Theatre*, taught me about the exciting issues involved when the actor co-creates the event of theater with the spectator. This co-creation is not an act of spectacle, but one of intimate communication within the moment of performance. This introduction to Grotowski, however, further opened yet another connection to a place that kept popping up in my life at the most unpredictable moment—Poland.

## Shifting Identities

In 1984, I received a very surprising note from the UWSP International Programs telling me I had been chosen to lead a group of students to Poland. Many Polish immigrants escaping World War II had settled in Stevens Point and the ties were still strong. Even though this request turned out to be a mistake (another L. Caldwell on campus was the intended recipient), in the end, due to sickness of the other faculty member, I found myself preparing to go to Poland with 30 students. This unintended opportunity led to 15 years of work at differing times and in various capacities throughout Poland. In these years, I found myself shifting identities between who I was as an American, a dancer, an educator, and a foreigner. At times, the shifts were calming like lilting lullabies; at other times, I felt precipices looming with each wild pendulum swing.

### Pieces of the Past

My name, Linda, becomes destabilized within the Polish language. Depending on the placement of Linda within a Polish sentence, I am Lindo, Lindu, Lindy, or Lindetchka (a term of endearment), fascinating, yet also a bit unsettling.

In 1985, after martial law had been lifted in Poland, our Wisconsin student exchange group arrived by train into Kraków and was promptly escorted to a somewhat dreary dormitory, our home during the semester-long stay at the Jagellonian University where we took daily courses in Polish language, art history, political history, and economics. Once established, and having found private people to exchange our program's dollars into złoty that had to be strapped to my waist at all times, I immediately began to ferret out the dance scene. During this search, I discovered that the only professional companies—that is, those sanctioned by the State with salaried dancers—worked in ballet or folk dance forms. Modern dance was given amateur or unpaid status and relegated to the numerous State-Supported Culture Houses (Dom Kultury) similar to American YMCAs. In Poland, young people were expected to participate in the various arts and language programs offered by the Culture Houses at the end of each school day. This dictum, interestingly, led to a finely tuned network of modern dancers developing within cities and towns all over Poland. During the summer vacations, these dancers would travel to dance workshops and performances supported by the various Culture Houses where rich and fertile soil was laid and in which contemporary Polish dance energies flourished. I witnessed this phenomenon as a living example of a grassroots movement.

## Unreal Spaces

In the late 1990s, as a doctoral student in dance research, I returned to Poland with tape recorder and camera to record the stories of various Polish dance artists and to visually document the dance festivals at the Baltic University in Gdańsk and the Silesian Dance Theatre in Bytom.

### Pieces of the Past

I sit on a couch with Polish dancers Wojciech Mochniej and Aurora Lubos. Wojciech had taken part in Culture House dance activities as a young boy while, at the same time, learning street dance from 1980s MTV videos brought in from Germany. He becomes one of the first dancers hired to be in Jacek Luminski's contemporary dance company, The Silesian Dance Theatre. Wojciech tells a story of dance emerging in an "unreal space":

> I like to look out the window while listening to the music—especially at night. I stick my head out the window and I know it is dark and silent and yet here is all this music in my head. It is this incredible experience of opposite . . . umm opposite stuff . . . these opposites, how they work together filling my head with images. It is how I like to see . . . by actively looking through opposite eyes. This is when I can begin to see dance in the unreal space. The space can change . . . I can question the traditional space. Something can shift, it can be redrawn in the imagination. (December 21, 1999)

Aurora Lubos then weaves in her own narration. She tells me about being schooled in the visual arts and dance and later performing with Wojciech Mochniej and Melissa Monteros, directors of W & M Physical Theatre currently based in Calgary, Canada. Aurora's story of a Polish imagination continues:

> Also when I am watching someone's work I see how the face is important for me. Not whether she is moving correctly but whether the face is working. If the movement is true, the face will show it. I think one way of working . . . which I do on myself . . . when we run a part of the whole

piece, is to try to do it fully . . . fully, fully, even just a small phrase. It
is to catch a set feeling. In repetition, when your body becomes tired,
then your body cannot lie. There are points when your energy should
change which are also important to me, where you have to bring whole
energy with you to the front and throw the energy to the audience . . . it
is a rebuilding. The rebuilding is like you show with your energy that
you are going crazy to do something, you don't know what or how it
should look . . . you have no idea. But you rebuild. (December 22, 1999)

Students from America had traveled with me and, together, we participated in activities, kept journals of our experiences, and created shared stories.

## Pieces from the Past

My students and I navigate our bumping luggage through a warren of small
booths spread out before the entrance to the Kraków Train Station where offer-
ings of a large variety of clothes, food, magazines, and electronic equipment
are spread out and actively hawked by sellers speaking diverse languages.
However, we keep our foci glued on the remodeled Baroque-styled train station while snaking around the numerous distractions. We climb the stairs to
the station, enter the open and bustling lobby, and rapidly peruse the large
marquis overhead directing us to the track (peron) of our train. We climb
up and down more steep stairways until we reach our track. We breathlessly
hope that the Polish announcements we hear over the loud speakers, but do
not understand, have nothing to do with changes to our train. Luckily, I spy
Iwona Olszowska, a Polish dancer rehearsing in Bytom with Risa Jaroslaw's
New York-based dance company, sitting on a bench waiting for our train.
I loudly call out to her in English (ignoring the irritated stares around me)
joyfully realizing we will have a Polish travel-mate to guide us on the train.
The train arrives and we all heave our luggage up the iron stairs and through
the narrow passageway looking for free seats. After settling in, we catch up
on our lives. The young Polish people in our compartment speak English and
periodically join our conversation, while the older Poles seated across from
us continue their dialogues in rapid Polish. In the midst of these conflicting
languages, food is offered all around and the little dog held by one of the
older Polish women is given her full share. This is a very different journey
than the isolated ones I make in my American car.

Narrow rows of green pastures pass by outside the train window. People
working in the fields ignore the train as do the solitary cows tethered to
iron stakes and the storks nesting on the tops of houses. Most of the houses
appear to be newly constructed from cement blocks with colorful patios
and shutters accenting gray, unpainted exteriors. Many seem caught in a

continual process of becoming—families living in one small section add cement extensions as family members and financial incomes fluctuate over time. We pass through small towns and stop at train stations now sporting newly uplifted faces, very different from the sagging demeanors observed during my earlier trips in the 1980s. As we approach Katowice, the major industrial center of the Silesian district, the landscape radically changes. Individual farms give way to Communist-era large, gray, concrete apartment complexes interspersed with 19th-century German buildings of solid red brick. All, however, are covered with a patina of black coal dust coming from the mostly inoperable factories perched like dragons in befouled lairs.

Once the train stops, we gather our belongings and disembark only to immediately run into a dancer and writer from Vilno, Lithuania. Iwona takes charge of us all as we fall in step with her brisk walk. We exit the train station and trek down the heavily populated pedestrian mall bumping our luggage animatedly along the cobble-stoned road passing the local McDonalds on our way. Glancing inside the yellow arches I notice that the interior is decorated with fine art prints. (McDonalds had to promise an artful presence to many Polish cities before they were allowed to build.) Iwona spies the bus we need and begins jogging toward it yelling over her shoulder that she will have the driver wait for us. We frantically jerk along, push our way onto the crowded bus, and nervously apologize as we jostle the standing riders trying to make room for us. We are let off in Bytom at a cabstand. I start toward the closest cab, but am stopped short by Iwona telling me firmly that we must only take a cab with a certain number, having to do with discounts, cards, phones, and a set of variables beyond my grasp. She chooses the third cab in line (which, from what I could see, had no discernible difference from the first one) and the driver miraculously fits our luggage and four of us into one car. Finally, we reach the theater housing our festival and find ourselves amidst fellow wandering dancers from Poland, Russia, Lithuania, Slovenia, Slovakia, Germany, Holland, Switzerland, and America.

## Imagined Play of Memory

On our return to the States, our journal entries about our Polish experiences became the frame for the format of my doctoral dissertation. The dissertation became an imaged play of memory in which I attempted to bring alive to the American reader the story of how a hidden, but now very present and complex, contemporary dance form was rearing, and always had reared, its head in Poland. While writing, I realized the Polish participants had, like the motel manager in my childhood dream, shared their pencils with me and the responsibility was mine to skillfully manipulate these pencils in order to open "listening spaces" in which the swirling voices of the Polish dancers could be heard. At times I felt I was successful, at other times, I could not get my fingers to animate the pencils in tandem with those desiring to be heard. I am still working on developing those skills as more pencils with differing shapes, textures, and weights are shared with me daily by the many dancers passing through my life.

In 2011, as I entered my 60s, I found myself the coordinator of the Texas Woman's University low-residential doctoral program. I sat in front of my computer reading the research of emerging doctoral students while also reflecting back on the 8-year-old girl at the beginning of this story as she dreams about documenting happenings taking shape around and within her. Along the way, I never guessed that at the end of my dance career I would once again be handed a pencil, a 21st-century pencil in the form of a keyboard, with which I could record the act of remembering those who shaped my dance journey. Yet, writing about dance, or discovering how to create a writing that moves with dance, continues to be a challenge. The beauty of memories, the movement of thoughts, no matter how difficult to catch in action, continue to energize my desire to take on that challenge—"a feat of mutual trust, of mutual imagining . . . pieces of the past that swim into the present" (p. 5).

## Reference

Roy-Bhattacharya, J. (2011). *The storyteller of Marrakesh*. New York: W. W. Norton.

------

# 8

# From the Floor to the Floor

## Melanie Ríos Glaser

### A Ticket to The Wooden Floor

Like Rice Krispies on a microphone, the high curved ceiling went snap, crackle, and pop as the wood expanded and contracted. The sound made me think that the top floor studios at The Wooden Floor were sighing and settling after a 6-hour rehearsal with more than 100 dancers aged 10 to 18 years. I lay on the studio floor on my back like a starfish. Starting my time in the studio space with my back on the floor and finishing there helps me come into myself, to arrive into the space and into my body, a ritual that created itself. In the past 6 years I have yearned to spend more time in the studio engaged in that cycle: from the floor to the floor.

My position as executive and artistic director of The Wooden Floor in Santa Ana, California, has dance as its center but does not necessarily translate into time in the studio for me. Slowly but steadily, I had turned away from the dance floor and become a nonprofit administrator. Meetings, emails, and luncheons occupied every working hour. I am still here because The Wooden Floor is a remarkable place. Children join between the ages of 8 and 13 and the organization commits to seeing them through to high school graduation in addition to offering college scholarships. At The Wooden Floor, youngsters immerse themselves in dance after school hours. All programs are free of charge. They call The Wooden Floor their second home. Only one caveat exists: They must come from a disadvantaged background to join. These students have more hurdles than most. Here they have space, a solid floor underneath them, and a community that supports the journey into adulthood.

Every October, children and their parents line up outside our building, some as early as 2 a.m., hoping that being the first in line will increase their chances to earn a spot. I hold back tears as I face the line that wraps itself around the block. Who am I to choose whose life is going to be deeply shaped by The Wooden Floor? Since 2005, all of our graduates finish high school on time and enroll in college, three times the national average for their socioeconomic peers! Dance can help break the cycle of poverty. We prove the power of dance every day. This past year, 364 children auditioned for about 70 slots to complete the student body of 375. Word has spread that a ticket to The Wooden Floor might just change everything. I was an independent freelance choreographer, improviser, and dance educator in 1997 when I met the founder of The Wooden Floor, Beth Burns, at the legendary Jacob's Pillow Dance festival. For me, that meeting did change everything.

## Juilliard and the Freelance Years

I graduated from The Juilliard School in 1994. Juilliard was simply Juilliard— the prestige alone was later going to serve as a booster engine serves a rocket ship. Not that I have made a full orbit but Juilliard helped. The chances of having trained in Guatemala and landing a spot at Juilliard were slim but with the University of California, Santa Barbara (UCSB) in between they got better. Indeed, my previous 2 years at UCSB had prepared me for Juilliard. I had an itch to transfer. UCSB felt large and I had gotten lost in the shuffle. I needed to decide between a better business school and a dance conservatory. I had been accepted conditionally in UC Berkeley's business program if I passed a calculus class that I had previously failed. For years I told a story that I had flipped a coin between Berkeley and Juilliard but the truth is that that summer I failed to pass the math course yet again. While retaking the calculus class a friend I had met in London came to visit. I chose to take a trip to Baja, California, rather than study calculus—that was the way I often made decisions then. I must have playfully tossed a coin at some point and unconsciously I came to incorporate that chance act into my narrative. The Juilliard years were intense as would be expected. I complained about the lack of exposure to the work happening in the downtown dance scene, feeling we were only being exposed to classical modern work. Nevertheless, I was in awe of the place and the legendary teachers that inhabited or visited the school.

On a trip to New York at the age of 11, as a special treat to see a class from the American Ballet Theatre, I had visited the very studio in which my audition for Juilliard would take place and later I would take daily classes. We were part of a tour group that had traveled specifically to see day after day of ballet performances. My parents were balletomanes. Baryshnikov was in the hallway talking to someone. I gathered my courage, approached him and upon asking for his autograph he ruffled my hair and said: "Another day honey." Another day? I had travelled all the way from Guatemala and here HE was! According to my ballet teacher I had been blessed; I had been touched. What touches me now is Baryshnikov's dedication to new dance, encouraging with his name and resources the creation of adventuresome work.

Early on in my career, before my years at The Wooden Floor, I made a decision that, for a decade, I would postpone thinking about my present and future financial well-being. Otherwise I was convinced I would not make art. By searching out opportunities such as grants, fellowships, and scholarships, I was able to string along a meager living, but most importantly I was making a life in dance—at least most of the time. One useful tactic was to keep no permanent home, which meant that my things were often packed in boxes at my parents' house and I would go from project to project. I was either being housed or was subletting and lived out of my suitcase. I learned to have a high tolerance for risk.

After graduating from Juilliard I stayed in New York for a few months. Determined to create my own work, I put together a project for a festival in Guatemala City and returned home to stage my first full evening production with a small company of four. This project led to work with the Ballet Moderno y Folklórico de Guatemala over the next 4 years and to the creation of my own company, The Mosquito Dance Company.

Creating and touring work in Latin America was an adventure. We showed up for our tech rehearsal at the National Theatre in El Salvador and the stage crew would not move until a televised soccer game ended. In Guatemala City they melted the dry ice in a frying pan on a brick with a heated coil. A man with a fan pushed the fog onstage in clumsy jerks. At that first production in Guatemala two guards decided to watch from an arch next to the stage built on some ruins and cast an enormous shadow with their rifles on the backdrop. With this image my work suddenly became political. At one matinee a stray dog walked with purpose across the stage and the children laughed. In Colombia, where I had been invited to start a modern dance wing to the Ballet de Cali, the studios were built outside the city on a farm with ducks, dogs, and cows that occasionally made their way into the space. We sometimes had to pick up their droppings in the early morning. We had an unforgettable tour through Central America. The air conditioning was broken in the theater in Panama City, and the theater in Managua had only pink lighting gels. In some places we danced on marley floors, if any, which were barely stitched together with pieces of scotch tape. In Panama City, the government censor, a short man with glasses and a clipboard, walked into the theater on a mission. He was there on the afternoon of opening night to make sure the work had no improprieties. One choreographer, fatigued with the prevalent "it can't be done" attitude, went ballistic and barked at him so loudly that he scurried away and our show went on stage without censorship (or improprieties.) The costumes got lost with the luggage and customs held our scenery hostage. No matter what, we went on dancing. We were nicknamed the four-wheel drive dancers. I had the time of my life.

The freelance life also allowed me to spend part of my year in Tangier, Morocco, with my partner at that time, Rodrigo Rey Rosa. He was and still is a well-known Central American writer. Always a welcomed break, I used the time to regroup, plan out new projects, and rest. Born and raised in Guatemala, I felt a sense of freedom living in another third world country that was not my own and for which I felt less responsibility. Because I was a foreigner, I could distance myself and observe. Having given up on learning Arabic past my most basic needs, I enjoyed being silent. The whole day could be spent walking down to the *medina* to buy oranges and water. We lived without a refrigerator or any electric appliances (other than an iron) in a nearly empty, whitewashed house on the top of the *Kasbah*. The house had a panoramic view of the city, the port, and ships. On a clear day, you could see all the way across this northern coast of Africa to the coast of Spain. I read voraciously from books borrowed from the library of Paul Bowles. Although he didn't like the title, Paul was often referred to as the father of the Beat Generation and had become a world-famous writer with the publication of his book *The Sheltering Sky* (1949). As a composer, he wrote music for Cunningham and the Marquis de Cuevas. Rodrigo was heir to Paul Bowles and we would spend the afternoons with Paul drinking mint tea. I prodded him to tell me about his travels and his famous modernist friends and collaborators such as writer Gertrude Stein, Tennessee Williams, composer Aaron Copland, and artist Salvador Dali. By spending time with Paul I felt I had a direct line to the modernist artists of his generation. He was one of several mentors who I would attach myself ferociously to during those formative years.

## A Chance Meeting at Jacob's Pillow

In June 1997 I boarded a ferry in Tangier to take me across the Strait of Gibraltar to Algeciras. Arriving with time to kill, I sat to rest my eyes on a round bench in the plaza of this unapologetic port city. Out of the corner of my eye I caught the hand of a youth aiming for my purse like a lizard's tongue to a fly. Avoiding a disaster he fled without his prize. A third-class train, stopping at every town, took me to Malaga and on to another crowded train where I was surrounded by soldiers smoking incessantly and joking crudely. I finally arrived in Madrid. I took a flight to Paris, and spent the night at a cheap airport hotel. The next day I was off to Philadelphia. Upon landing, I inhaled with pleasure the smell of the United States. During my childhood in Guatemala we made occasional trips to Florida, and as I stepped out of the airplane and into the terminal of the Miami airport, a distinct smell permeated the air that I have always come to associate with the United States. To me the smell was of things that were new. I now suspect the scent was the carpet. The flight from Philadelphia to Boston was short and I arrived late to spend the night with a friend. She took me to the bus depot the next day and 2 hours later I was dropped off at Jacob's Pillow in the small town of Lee, Massachusetts. The trip had taken 4 days.

Through a blind video jury I had been one of nine artists selected from the Americas to receive a fellowship of $25,000 as part of a short-lived initiative of the Kennedy Center in Washington, DC. We were to use the money to further our art in the United States. Part of my plan was to take a choreography workshop at Jacob's Pillow with Bessie Schonberg. Bessie Schonberg had greatly advanced dance in higher education by establishing the Dance Department at Sarah Lawrence College in 1938, which inspired the creation of other dance departments across the country. She was considered one of the most influential choreography teachers of her generation. She had overseen my senior project at Juilliard; a work inspired by avant-garde Italian filmmaker Federico Fellini, *I Clowns* (1970). I remember Bessie walking toward me for the meeting in which she would critique my project. From a distance, her scarf looked a dark silk with golden emblems. We sat down and what she said next came as a shock and was a lesson that has stayed with me to today. She scolded: "My dear, you were not outrageous enough!" This woman in her late 80s was telling *me* that I had not gone far enough? Her declaration was particularly painful because I thought of myself as the risk taker, the one making the work on the edge. As I looked down, I noticed that the golden emblems on her scarf were not naval themed at all, they were creepy insects of all sorts. To this day I ask myself: "Am I pushing the envelope? Do I feel enough discomfort to know that I am treading into the difficult and the juicy? Am I wearing the scarf with the insects or something you buy at Brooks Brothers?"

A van picked me up in Lee, Massachusetts, to take me to Jacob's Pillow. A dancer in the van said: "Isn't it so sad that Bessie died?" The people at the desk said they had tried to reach me with the news to give me the chance to cancel but had been unable to locate me. I was, to an extent, willingly incommunicado in Morocco. Liz Keen was going to lead the workshop instead. Liz was dear to me and had been my composition teacher for more than 2 years at Juilliard. She had taught me well, but I had come to work with Bessie knowing that her time was limited. I wanted to practice being outrageous enough.

I sat on the edge of the bed with my head in my hands in the austere cabin where we were to live for the next 3 weeks. While I was feeling pity for myself, my roommate entered and sat across the bed from me looking distraught. She had been trying without success to get her own room and was none too happy to have to share. She introduced herself as Beth Burns and took off to petition for a single room one more time. Liz Keen agreed that I could do my own thing since I had studied 2 years with her. I decided to stay. Making work during those 3 weeks was like squeezing juice out of a raisin. I produced enough nuggets to catch the attention of Beth Burns who had settled into having me as her roommate. Beth had been focused on building what she described to me as a "little program for inner-city kids in Santa Ana, California." I think I helped her feel comfortable among the crowd of modern dancers. We were all intrigued by her 14 years as a Catholic nun for the Sisters of Saint Joseph of Orange. Beth left the convent in 1989 after deciding that life was no longer the right match for her.

## Beth Burns (Her Story)

From what I recall of Beth's story, the sisters in those days were deployed mostly to teach school children and she did not enjoy this much. During her years as a "nunny bunny," as she calls the sisters with affection, she knew that if she could teach dance, a passion she had cultivated during her years as a student at Loyola Marymount College, she could be of greater service to the community. Beth launched her pilot program in 1983 to help youth avoid their default future of gangs, poverty, and teenage pregnancy. She started teaching a handful of low income, mostly Latino youth in the basement of the Episcopal Church of the Messiah in downtown Santa Ana, California. With their first concert at the police annex, her company, then called Saint Joseph Ballet and now The Wooden Floor, was launched. Beth's choreography was inspired by the dignity and identity of these young people. Her predominant movement language was ballet and she made original work with a great instinct for theater. She thought creating current and relevant work was important to the mission of The Wooden Floor and that led her to commission work from me and subsequently other choreographers whose aesthetics were not ballet-based.

Beth: brilliant, strategic, informed, remarkable and determined. In those early years Beth did everything. She taught, fundraised, mentored, and managed. The Wooden Floor went from being housed in the church basement to a single studio and in a dramatic growth spurt she led the organization's move into new 21,455 square foot state-of-the-art studios and offices. With this, the organization incorporated academic and social service programs. Currently, in addition to the intensive dance education program The Wooden Floor's academic services provide one-on-one tutoring, reading programs, and remedial courses. Starting in the seventh grade, the organization guides students on the path to apply and enroll in college. The scholarship programs offer financial assistance to alumni in college. The services for families take the form of workshops, counseling, and crisis intervention. In order to retain the young dancers, we help the families overcome challenges such as hunger, eviction, joblessness, abuse, and mental health issues, to name a few of their many struggles. In the midst of this Capital Campaign to build the new campus, Beth had taken some professional development time to attend the choreography workshop at Jacob's Pillow.

Beth and I lost touch over the next couple years. In 1999, a letter that had been sent to an address in Guatemala made its way to me in New York. I was spending time with my long-time mentor and composition teacher Doris Rudko. Doris was a disciple of Louis Horst, although she had continued to evolve alongside the development of modern dance in her approach to teaching choreography. Apparently, Beth had assigned someone on her staff to find me hell or high water. With effort, they found me, which was not easy before Google or Facebook. I was invited to explore the possibility of creating a new work for The Wooden Floor. The invitation specified that I would be her "assistant" for the week of the concert. The "assistant" bit was actually a disguised audition to test my ability to establish some rapport with the students, most of them teenagers. I tried to make myself useful in any way I could and ended up mediating some strain between Beth's attention to detail and the laid back style of the Latin Jazz band she had hired. I passed the test and was invited to return to set a new piece. Perhaps what attracted her to my work was an inventive movement vocabulary and, for audiences less familiar with contemporary dance, I offered an entry through my exploration of physical humor.

## Choreographing for The Wooden Floor

My cast included 100 or so of the younger dancers. I had no clue as to what I was going to do and my very few experiences teaching children in the past had yielded mixed results. Here they were, sitting on the studio floor, looking at me with curiosity and waiting for instructions. I took roll. Ninety-eight percent of the names were Latino and, hoping to impress them, I pronounced them in my native Spanish. I would read off the list a name like Jorge (hor-hay) and the boy would say, "It's George." When the next one came around I would say "George" and the boy would say, "No it's Jorge." This happened several times and I glimpsed just how much I had to learn about this community.

In the years leading to my work with The Wooden Floor I had turned my attention to the multiplicity of approaches to improvisational dance including contact improvisation. Contact Improvisation, a dance form initiated by American choreographer Steve Paxton in 1972, is based on the communication between two or more moving bodies that are in physical contact. Attuned to gravity, momentum, and inertia, I once heard Contact Improvisation described as being similar to wrestling except that you use your force to help rather than hinder your opponent. The practice of Contact Improvisation, in addition to a brief stint of two summers as a guest artist with the dance company Pilobolus, had placed partnering at the center of my work. At one of my first rehearsals after trying arduously to find unusual lifts—"too much effort for such little effect" to quote Robby Barnett of Pilobolus—a young dancer said to me: "I can teach you a much easier way to lift someone." Such was the first of many comments from the young dancers that I would keep in my pocket to pull out for laughs over the years. My interest in "improvisational scores," which can be defined as the rules of the game or set of directions that structure an improvisation, also was useful. These scores can be restrictive, wide open, or anywhere in between. I find watching an improvisational score shape the action and the variations that come from the executors fascinating.

For my first work at The Wooden Floor, I divided the young dancers into groups and put them into motion by giving them some movement triggers. These directives that precipitate a new step or phrase can be as simple as "invent a new way to walk," or "create a machine with five friends." We created something akin to a playground where we made up games with rules, sometimes broke them or often misunderstood them. From there, movement ideas emerged. I had learned at clown school, which I also paid for with the Kennedy Center grant, that in order to protect yourself from messages from above, having something on top of your head, such as a hat, feather, or a dot painted on with magic marker, was important. Coming to rehearsal with my short hair in a little fountain at the top of my head like that of a 6-month-old seemed to break the ice with the kids. My fountain also gave me a boost of energy and protected me in case anything did decide to come from above or the side or below.

The ending emerged based on a series of high-speed runs across the stage, where dancers dropped and others jumped over them and then another group of 50 ran and froze, dropped, jumped, and ran faster. The movement was thrilling. Beth walked into the studio and looked worried as she saw me yelling at all 100 kids to run faster, faster, faster, as they went in and out of the wings with ferocity. To Beth's credit she only expressed her concern for their safety to my rehearsal director Rebeca Ramos. Rebeca was to be the brilliant logistician who, for the next 10 years, would make my choreographic ideas come to life without serious accidents. We called the dance *All Heaven Broke Loose*. After a dress rehearsal of this piece at the Irvine Barclay Theatre, I met Brian, my future husband, another way in which that chance encounter with Beth shaped my life. He walked up to me and eloquently praised the work. He had just finished his PhD in English at Berkeley and occasionally published poems. If you want to woo me, give me thoughtful praise of my work—that's where my vanity lies.

Beth was to do a piece for the older dancers but she continued to be overwhelmed with the responsibilities of the growing organization and so she commissioned a second work from me that year. Between 2000 and 2005, I came back almost annually. Somewhere along the way, Beth started to think about retiring and naming me the heir apparent. Beth had redefined a role for the new artistic director much along the lines of what she dreamed her job could eventually become, with less focus on the executive, administrative, and fundraising responsibilities and more time for furthering the artistic ambitions of the organization. As a child, I played supermarket and spent hours making the money, drawing up checkbooks, creating a shelf full of pretend food, and setting up the cash register. When all that was done, I no longer wanted to play. In similar fashion, Beth built a stellar organization with blood and tears, defined her dream role, and then offered the position to me.

## From Europe to Orange County

In 2002, Brian and I individually applied for Fulbright scholarships, a program of competitive grants for international educational exchange for students, scholars, teachers, professionals, scientists, and artists. This is a good option for recent graduates or mid-career artists. Originally, the idea that both of us would be given scholarships seemed a long shot. We both received them and, of course, neither of us wanted to turn the offer down. After our wedding in Guatemala, we headed toward Europe with the intent of commuting between Paris, France, where I was based, and Düsseldorf, Germany, where he would be teaching. We had 6 weeks to spend together before I was due in Paris. We were sent to the cold outpost of Kiel on the northernmost tip of Germany for a language-immersion program. My grammar teacher was so stern that when I mispronounced a word he would instantly yell "Nein!" For the second time, I gave up on learning another language. I was there to learn, not to build character.

While in Kiel, a fateful message arrived from Beth asking me to succeed her as the second artistic director for The Wooden Floor. She wanted to retire in June 2005. Because of the trepidation as to how the organization was going to survive without Beth, the transition and planning phase took well over a year. During this time, I often heard the phrases "big shoes to fill," "hard act to follow," and "there is only one Beth Burns." I responded by saying that I would have to do because that's who you have right now. Beth was getting married and starting, in her own words, the second half of her life. Growing The Wooden Floor from a small startup nonprofit to a model organization had taken tremendous amounts of dedication and energy. She must have felt tired.

I found turning down the offer impossible. The appointment was aligned with my passions and meant some stability as we planned to start a family. Moving to Orange County, California, was not only where The Wooden Floor was located but also where my husband's family lived. That was a good thing; the bad thing was that Orange County, with few exceptions, is almost barren of any adventuresome art making. In the window of time before we made the move to Orange County, our daughter Andoe was born. After having been in 10 countries during her stay in my womb because of our nomadic lifestyle—a bit of an exaggeration as I am counting just passing through the small ones like Luxembourg—Andoe was born in Germany in 2004. In the first few months of her life, we traveled back and forth from Düsseldorf to Santa Ana so that I could restage some of Beth's work in my own voice, a visible gesture of passing the baton. I also was tasked with earning the confidence of the Board of Directors and donors.

The first day of work, I walked into the artistic director's office and on my chair was a black and white photograph of me that Beth had out as a welcome. She had left a month earlier. Where was the manual on how to be the artistic director of a large arts-for-youth organization? My charge was "to move the art forward." The glitch here was that all staff, with the exception of one person, reported to the executive director and the morale of the team was low. This fact, in addition to my inexperience, left me little agency to make things happen. Eight months later the executive director resigned.

Thus, a few months into the job I found myself, albeit with a helpful Board of Directors, in charge of the whole enchilada, at least temporarily. I knew the difference between a balance sheet and an income statement, but barely. As usual, I thought a book would be helpful. At night I read every book on nonprofit management that I could find. Professional development workshops, webinars and peer groups helped. After some time, I was deeply invested in nonprofit management. We grew the budget to $2.4 million a year, of which 90% had to be raised from individual donors, foundations, and corporations. Raising money is how I would spend much of my time.

At this point, the Board of Directors hired a consulting firm to do an assessment of the organization, make a recommendation for the right structure, and lead a national search for the next managing director. Hiring the right people and forming a good team was the most critical and challenging part of leadership for me. We hired a person who was the wrong fit for our organization. For the next year, I was to co-lead this organization alongside her. She did eventually resign. Fortunately, the financial structure of The Wooden Floor is strong and its donors loyal. Over time, this became a blip in the organization's timeline, although for me the whole process had made my hair begin to turn gray.

I was pregnant with our son John, and my husband was ill for several months when all this was happening. Fortunately, having been converted to psychoanalysis in the early 2000s, my analyst, Gabrielle Schwab, walked with me during all those difficult years. On that couch I had the space to regroup, growl, and rock myself into staying present.

At this point, I just wanted to take over at The Wooden Floor. I made a suggestion already in the minds of many on the Board that we consolidate the position of the executive and artistic director and threw my hat in the ring for the job. I am in my seventh year with The Wooden Floor full time. Things have gotten easier as I grow accustomed to the numerous speaking engagements, working under pressure, and the pure grit required to ask for money. I don't work 55 to 65 hours a week anymore nor does the job completely consume me. I am more present for my children.

## Disconnecting

A year ago, the Board of Directors granted me a 3-month sabbatical. By this time, the general manager and chief financial officer (CFO), Dawn Reese, already had assumed many major responsibilities in the organization. Finding and hiring Dawn made all the difference. I did not check into company email, voicemail, nothing. No possible case scenario could bring me out of my sabbatical except for a major death. I completely retracted.

My sabbatical started with a week by the ocean with my kids. I later cloistered myself for 6 days at a retreat center in northern California where

I wrote 100 pages through a guided journaling process for 8 hours a day. What I found inside was anger and a profound sadness. I felt as if I had been robbed of the first year of my son's life. With just so much work to do to keep The Wooden Floor moving forward, I had had no real maternity leave. I returned to the West Coast Improvisation Dance Festival for a few days and saw old friends. I spent some time puttering around my house, finding lost parts of toys underneath the furniture, picking up my daughter from camp, or making up time with my son John. We all travelled to Guatemala for a month. There, I was being recruited to run a phenomenal nonprofit organization that helps the young people who live in the community around the city garbage dump. This was life in poverty as I had never before witnessed. Living conditions were abominable. They took me on a tour under pouring rain through one of the many shantytowns built on trash and toxic substances, next to the city's cemetery. The deep melancholy I feel living somewhere other than Guatemala does not abate. Here was a viable opportunity to return.

Even my family, who voluntarily live in Guatemala City, advised me against the move as things were not going well politically and the country was still a dangerous place to live, even more so than when I grew up during the civil war. During those years, the horrific violence was perhaps more targeted, and on occasion ideologically driven. Complex as the decision was, I made my choice. I decided my work at The Wooden Floor was not done and I did not want to distance myself from art making even more than I had.

## Mind Map

My sabbatical ended with a 3-day retreat up the coast of California. In Pelican Bay, I laid out a mind map as I was dining by myself in the hotel restaurant. Clearly, the map pointed to spending more time as a practicing artist. I felt satisfaction in my accomplishments as an executive director but when people defined me that way I felt misperceived. I enjoy pro bono consulting for other nonprofits on issues of nonprofit management, governance, fundraising, and programming. As artistic director, I lay out an aesthetic point of view for The Wooden Floor by commissioning work from choreographers who are shaping the genre of contemporary dance now. They are adventuresome and experimental in their approach and this has become a trademark of The Wooden Floor. Our risk-taking work has garnered us visibility amongst the dance community. Collaborating artists now include Mark Haim, Sean Curran, Sally Silvers, Nami Yamamoto, Susan Rethorst, John Heginbotham, Chris Yon, and Steve Paxton. The lighting designer, Jim Ingalls, preceded me, and remains a sun around which we all revolve. The year 2010 saw collaboration with the Merce Cunningham Dance Company and the video artist Bill Viola.

I took a full year after the revelations from my sabbatical to put forth a plan. The proposal was to return to a dual-leadership system that would name our general manager and CFO to the executive director position and get me back to where I started as artistic director. From the floor to the floor, the time and actions I invested in art-making ventures worked in direct or indirect benefit to The Wooden Floor, ensuring my vitality and our appeal to funders seeking leading-edge nonprofits. The plan allowed for my energies to be directed toward "moving the art forward." In November 2011, the Board of Directors approved my proposal. I am today officially the artistic director of The Wooden Floor. I am relieved of some responsibilities associated with the position of the executive director and given 8 to 10 weeks in order to be able to take outside commissions and produce my own work, independently of what I create for The Wooden Floor. I hope that with this new mind map, I will avoid a life I might regret by turning toward what is more aligned with my inner passions, hopes, and ambitions.

With a few projects here and there, I never completely stopped producing work in dance. I certainly made many pieces for student casts of hundreds. I made enough to have choreography trickle out like a leaking faucet. Revitalizing a career as a practicing artist by getting back in the studio and producing work is a daunting task. My body has changed. I am abreast of new trends but can I make work like the movement artists whose work I admire? I am terrified that my scarf will look as if bought at Brooks Brothers. I fear that my creative muscle has atrophied from spending so much time in my left brain.

I find myself committed and recommitted to dance anyway. The arts are my centering force. People ask me how I do it all and I usually answer, "I don't." Can one do it all and have it all? Twyla Tharp says she made a mistake thinking she could have it all. Can I have a family with two young children, a job working for a stellar nonprofit organization that helps low-income youth through dance, a career as a practicing artist, and a place or country that feels like home? Probably not. We recently returned a puppy after 3 weeks; cute as he was we could not handle the demands. The beds will sometimes go unmade. I will stumble into rehearsal without having prep time. John might be eating M&Ms when he gets up at 5 a.m., because 5 a.m. is too darn early to make breakfast. I will slow down a process at The Wooden Floor because a pertinent email is stuck in my inbox. Orange County continues to be somewhat isolated from the experimental work happening elsewhere and I will still miss Guatemala.

I have learned to build a life in dance with pieces. No more all or nothing. My energy is directed into multiple buckets, and something is better than nothing. Now, how can I be both prudent and keep my tolerance for risk? Most importantly, how do I keep those insects around my neck and move from floor to floor?

9

# Recipe for a Dance Artist

## Teoma Naccarato

### To Be a Dance Artist

*To be a dance artist, you must believe in yourself.* I have received a lot of rejection letters. I keep them in a shoebox in my closet to remind me how difficult and humbling pursuing a career in dance is. At the same time, these early rejections allow me to gauge my incremental advances over the years, which in addition to the odd leap or bound, amount to more tangible progress. When I encounter an obstacle in my path to dance—instability, insecurity, injury—I resist the crumbling feeling in my bones. Resistance is very useful for pushing forward with greater strength and clarity of direction. I ground myself, and use the barrier in front of me as a tool to strengthen my art and myself.

    *To be a dance artist, you must create dance.* And keep creating dance. And then create some more. I employ the term *dance artist* broadly, as defined in the introduction to this book, to include all people who commit over many years to "moving with aesthetic intention." The first piece I presented on stage was a female duet set to Sinead O'Connor, and the choreography was hyper-melodramatic. My second attempt was not so hot either. But 15 years later, I appreciate these early building blocks in my creative process. Each piece I produce, whether my ego labels the choreography *good* or *bad*, informs subsequent endeavors. My creative process is not confined within a

single project, but rather threads over, through and under my every intention and action as a creator.

*To be a dance artist, you must be a breathing, laughing, sweating, cry-
ing, screaming, and real person.* We are what we do. We do what we are. As
Ann Bogart (2001) states: "You cannot hide; your growth as an artist is not
separate from your growth as a human being: it is all visible" (p. 118). Over
time, dance has become for me not only a practice relevant in the studio or
stage, but my way of being, knowing, and interacting in the world.

## The Recipe

1 pint of vulnerability
10 gallons of intimacy
100 drops of uncertainty
Combine and mix well

For me, being a dance artist demands vulnerability, intimacy, and
uncertainty on and off stage. These ingredients define the texture, scent, and
flavor of my creations and collaboration with colleagues, mentors, family,
friends, and lovers, many of whom wear several hats at once. In my practice,
vulnerability entails exposing my soft spots—emotionally, mentally, physically—in order to turn up the dial and burn out the salmonella of fear, guilt,
or shame. Vulnerability is a process of facing myself, complete with insecurity,
anger, pain, anxiety, loss, desire, ego, and so much more—but gently, with
recognition that I am formed from the inside-out and outside-in. Intimacy
involves moving toward vulnerability with others—seeing, hearing, smelling, tasting, and holding each other, even if only for a moment. Uncertainty
means letting go each day of what I imagine I know or control about my art,
my partner, and myself. No formula exists for creation, relationships, or life.
No recipe yields identical results twice, at least not for me. But my hunger is
incessant, so I continue to cook up and chew on dance, filling my belly with
sweet, sour, and spicy sustenance. My goal is not to become a Cordon Bleu,
but rather the mother of a soup kitchen, sharing and devising in a hungry
community. To be a dance artist, I toss in all of the vulnerability, intimacy,
and uncertainty I can muster and stir well, forming the batter from which
nutritious and delicious dances are prepared.

## 1 Pint of Vulnerability

Three years of long distance . . . we talk on the phone, but video chatting makes
me miss him more. Something about the pixilated, tinted materialization of

my lover on screen reinforces his absence. I crave his touch, smell, taste, and warmth. My imagination conjures a more substantive connection than a fleeting, virtual representation of his presence. My most recent creation, *Gently between us,* found seed in the fertile vulnerability, intimacy, and uncertainty of my long-term, long-distance relationship. By manipulating four cameras on stage, the dancers connect and depart in flesh and video projection, negotiating geographical and emotional distance. As the creative process in *Gently between us* grew, my narrative of mediated love became entwined with stories from collaborators, as well as social and political concerns regarding embodiment and technology. The movement between personal, communal, and social concerns in *Gently between us* exemplifies my overall approach to creation and pedagogy. My personal experiences, beliefs, and behaviors are profoundly linked to the people, places, history, and culture in which I live. By investigating and sharing what makes me feel vulnerable on and off stage, I hope to create an intimacy that invites others to do the same.

As a choreographer and pedagogue, I desire for the creative process in every project I direct to be engaging, challenging, and relevant to my collaborators. I aim to offer space for growth, health, and development individually, and as a community. The construction of *Gently between us* necessarily involved therapy, healing, and community building, without which I do not believe we could have crafted a product that would touch audiences as deeply. I see aspects of myself and each of the performers in the final piece, but we are exaggerated, morphed, framed, and treated in ways that stretch and transform the possibilities of who and how we are. *Gently between us* is not a representation of relationships in my own life, or of those between the cast, but it does draw on the energy and emotion of real-life experiences. By connecting to potent personal memories but letting go of individual storylines, I collaborate with a team to lay fodder for creation.

Given the vulnerable character of my creative process, membranes between personal and professional relationships are often porous. Time and again I find myself attracted to collaborating with close friends. In my view, our pre-established trust, communication, and ability to negotiate conflict deepen our engagement in the studio. In turn, artistic investigations expand our comprehension of one another in social interactions. My best friend has performed in my choreography for more than 10 years, and I feel that the synergy and candidness with which we operate deepens the quality of our creative research. When I work with a new dancer, or a group of dancers who do not know each other, the initial phase of our process emphasizes trust building on a physical, emotional, and intellectual level, bringing us closer as artists and individuals. For this reason, I value working with collaborators over a long period of time.

The original cast of *Gently between us* included dancers with whom I had collaborated for nearly a year on previous projects. Gradually, we were moving together toward vulnerability via exercises that stimulate somatic sensing, memory, and imagination, as well as trust and community. Practices such as Authentic Movement, Theatre of the Oppressed, Contact Improvisation, and Gaga Movement Language informed our performative dialogue between personal and political, life and art, emotional and rational, and practice and theory. I sensed that we were developing rich support and openness in the group to venture into sensitive territory surrounding the theme of mediated intimacy. We began to explore nuance of touch in quality and intention, ranging from delicate tracing to abrasive grasping. At moments I perceived choreographic tension and conflation between desirable versus unwanted contact. Via zoom, angle, framing, and lighting, the penetrating eye of the video camera revealed and transformed intricacies in the dancers' interactions.

The process was surging along, until a dancer quit. Losing a dancer from the project halted me in my tracks. She stated that she was uncomfortable with the hyper-sexuality in the piece as it conflicted with her religious beliefs. I was shocked. In an entire year of striving to facilitate safe space for dialogue, risk, and experimentation, how could I have been unaware of what she was feeling? In rehearsals I had explicitly stated my desire to prioritize personal boundaries. Had I pushed too far? I recognized that I was taking her decision very personally, and a counter-narrative in my mind stressed that I should maintain professional distance from the situation. After all, this was a severed *professional* relationship, not a *personal* one, right? I could find another dancer and the project would continue as planned. But for me, moving forward was not that simple. In my experience, any meaningful relationship on or off stage necessitates trust as the platform from which to dive toward deep vulnerability. I have no interest in facilitating a detached and impersonal process because if what my collaborators and I create does not touch and move us, why would it matter to anyone else? The material with which this dancer was uncomfortable had emerged from her through structured improvisation, and I felt that the movements were personal and specific to her. As such, when she left the project, the persona and material we had developed for her disappeared from the piece, necessitating critical aesthetic and thematic changes.

This experience illuminated for me the significance of trust in my collaborative relationships on a personal and professional level. I felt judged and rejected by a dancer at an early stage in my process, which snowballed into insecurities regarding what other collaborators or an audience of my peers, family, and strangers might interpret about me based on my work. Despite much reassurance from the group, for a good month I felt lost and embarrassed to push boundaries in ways that might make the remaining cast uncomfortable. I was tiptoeing through rehearsal, and asking permission for each new directive. I realized that the trust-building process that I facilitate in my projects is as much for me as for the performers. In the absence of trust, vulnerability was becoming a destructive force in my process. Out of fear, I began to focus primarily on mechanics of movement material, and technical aspects of video and technology. The movement became polished and comfortable by way of repetition. I spent excessive time analyzing the piece through writing, and preparing for rehearsal in stringent detail. I was trying to understand and control—perhaps even tame—the meaning and content of the piece. *Gently between us* began in a potent, personal place, but through my fear and embarrassment had transformed into a detached portrayal of experiences. The piece was dying, and at that point, probably not worth sharing.

During this period, one of my project advisors came to rehearsal to give feedback. She had many positive and constructive comments, but the one that affected me most deeply, and helped me immensely, was that the piece wasn't making her *feel* anything yet. Emotional responses are subjective, but I too felt distant from the piece. Days later, I met with another advisor who asked what my vision for the project was in regard to sharing with an audience. What did I want to offer or leave the audience with? My answer was clear; I wanted to engage the audience emotionally based on their own experiences of intimacy in live and virtual relationships. I wanted to make them feel something personal, honest, and raw, below the surface of emotional stability and certainty that so often are projected by individuals in our culture. I wanted my vulnerability as a creator, and that of the performers, to give the audience permission to acknowledge, explore, and possibly even share their own desires, fears, and realities of solitude, dependency, and mediated love. Through these reflections, I realized that in order to create a raw and vulnerable piece, I had to be open to a raw and vulnerable process.

At this juncture I urged myself to disregard the looming pressure of the premiere, which made me want to package up my piece and shoot down the express route to the finish line. I saw no point in arriving, or even embarking, with materials that did not matter to me. Instead, I wandered back roads, dedicating time at the start of each rehearsal to trust-building activities. I led and participated in improvisations that involved "witnessing" a partner moving and speaking, weight-sharing, attention to touch, memory visualizations, and much more. We retraced and repaved avenues of support within the group. Gradually, I recovered my voice in the project and shaved veneer from the movement vocabulary that had become mechanical and safe through over-analysis and replication. By restoring trust and community in the group, we made space for vulnerability both on and off stage. We relit the engine for creation, and our process resurged.

In many years of creating dance, this is the project in which I most fully let go, with reasserted effort each day, of making a piece that I thought the

audience would like. Although I never created to please others intention-
ally, in the name of accessibility a polished sheen seemed to seep over my
final products. I believe that ego, and the need for approval in an evaluative
sense, will hold me back from the deep vulnerability required to connect with
people in art and life. One reason that I returned to school for my master's
in fine arts in dance was to create in a noncommercial setting where I could
risk failing. I wanted to be able to make a piece, or many pieces, that were
not necessarily popular or liked, but that could speak to people in other
ways. I needed time and space to question my choreographic process, voice,
and identity. I craved a supportive community in which I could risk being
personally and professionally vulnerable.

## 10 Gallons of Intimacy

I often begin rehearsal with a simple exercise of intimacy:

> In pairs, stand facing each other as close together as feels comfortable.
> Close your eyes and focus internally on breath circulating from the lungs;
> the temperature of skin and air; dull aches and pains; gravity pouring
> down a limb. Scan head to toe, situating yourself in this specific time
> and space. Once you are grounded, try to sense the palpable, energetic
> presence of the partner inches in front of you. When you grasp concretely
> his/her company, open your eyes. This will occur at different moments
> for each partner. Without losing the kinesthetic hum between you, add
> eye contact to the equation. Look deeply at each other. Really see him/
> her, for a sustained time, and let him/her see you. If you giggle, or laugh
> hysterically, just keep looking and connecting and returning focus to
> your breath. Do this until you are no longer embarrassed, uncomfort-
> able, or insecure.

Intimacy is not something one can fake in the performance of dance.
Trust must be present in the creative process itself, enabling risk and experimentation between collaborators. Bogart (2001) comments: "What you do
in rehearsal is visible in the product. The quality of the time spent together
is visible" (p. 120). Earlier in this chapter, I described intimacy as "moving
toward vulnerability with others—seeing, hearing, smelling, tasting, and
holding each other." A Japanese proverb states: "First know yourself, then
know others." As a creator, I search internally in order to connect outward
with my collaborators, our subject matter, and eventually an audience.

When I enter the studio in a bad mood—angry, stressed, depressed,
anxious—and hide my state from the group (or even myself!), I eliminate my
potential to create anything sincere. Leaving my personal life at the door is

not desirable or possible. To do so is a short cut to creator's block. My very ability to connect my present state to the individuals, communities, and cultures with whom I engage via dance is meaningful and inspiring. That said, what I do slam the studio door shut on is any dead-end storylines pacing my mind (e.g., "I can't believe he said that and what have I done and how could this happen to me and my back hurts and I don't want to be here right now and . . ."). Once safely inside, I take a deep breath and try to harness the energy of my present emotions as a source for creation. I peer in my partner's eyes and let her look at me, each of us complete with fear, insecurity, anger, pain, anxiety, loss, desire, and ego. We see each other, vulnerable, so that we can begin to be moved.

When I started *Gently between us,* the central theme was isolation. As we rooted this topic in personal experience, our collective interest shifted to intimacy. I see isolation and intimacy as linked on a gradient of human experience—I cannot know one without also meeting the other. In her TED (Technology, Entertainment, Design) talk "The Power of Vulnerability," Brené Brown (2011) observes: "When you ask people about love, they tell you about heartbreak. When you ask people about belonging, they'll tell you their most excruciating experiences of being excluded. And when you ask people about connection, the stories they tell you are about disconnection." This principle of opposition is at play in my creations.

During the first 2 months of *Gently between us,* I worked in the studio to generate movement material with the dancers surrounding the polar theme of isolation-intimacy. Taking muse from the charged interpersonal relationships in German choreographer Pina Bausch's work, I adopted dance theater tactics to develop gestural motifs into solos and duets. For example, the dancers improvised in pairs surrounding the theme of "tough love." I was intrigued by the potential contradiction present in the intention to care for yet pressure someone. As each duo improvised, I identified key gestures or ways of touching and manipulating a partner that caught my attention. I let my immediate emotional and kinesthetic responses guide a first layer of choices. Step by step we narrowed the vocabulary of the duets by delineating shape, spatial pathways, dynamic shifts, and more. We auditioned different developments of each duet over time through phrasing, accumulation, repetition, isolation, transposition, and diminution. We also experimented with the dancers speaking to one another and the audience, giving verbal directives such as "touch me," "hold me," "want me," "stop," "more," "again," "harder." We explored obstacles to emotional, physical, and psychological intimacy in a direct manner.

Over time, decipherable gestures morphed into idiosyncratic and gross motor choreography. Text gave way to audible breath and sound. Everything literal became more abstract, yet more potent. Importantly, the emerging nebulous forms were still rooted in concrete origins. For me, the swing toward abstraction gained momentum during the development of a solo for one of the female dancers, Cheryl. Initially, Cheryl stood at the microphone hissing commands at the group such as: "look," "touch," "come," "here," now," and exposing body parts as if to seduce or attract attention. I aimed to access a sense of desperation and loss of control in her persona, but with each run she seemed to me to be in charge of the group. I felt that her character was using sexuality (via nudity, posture, tone, etc.) to manipulate and gain power. This was not a female stereotype that I wanted to invoke or reinforce without question.

One night alone in the studio, I attempted to embody Cheryl's material to problem solve what might be holding the solo back. I realized that the directives I was giving her—to tell the others she wanted them with her words, gestures, and nudity—did not communicate severe thirst for intimacy. When I am emotionally or intellectually parched, solid words are not what I crave. Over the course of an hour-long improvisation, I searched in my body for the vulnerability that can arise from desire for attention, yet a simultaneous inability to accept care. The solo became about a physical and emotional state of being, from which movement and breath patterns emerged. I developed a specific evolution of movement with high contrast in dynamics between sensuality and aggression. I imagined a dark, confined space, and detailed my use of focus and breath. The next day I taught Cheryl this solo move by move with specified phrasing, points of initiation, and movement weight qualities. This approach was a major change from the improvisational directives I had been using to encourage exploration in her solo. In this instance, I observed that having a solid frame to push against enabled Cheryl to let go of more control emotionally, intellectually, and physically. Grasping the skeleton provided, she fleshed out details in movement quality, phrasing and body attitude, accessing performative qualities that were unexpected and unfamiliar behavior for her character, surprising even me.

Through candid embodied dialogue regarding both of our experiences of intimacy and isolation, I feel that Cheryl and I were able to step into one another's perspectives. This connection occurred at different points in the process with all of my collaborators. By experiencing vulnerability together in the creative process, my collaborators and I achieved a state of intimacy that infused our interactions on and off stage. I believe the quality of this connection was perceptible to the audience, who can sense the difference between "being" and "acting" in performance. I hope that by taking the risk of sharing my own vulnerability with the audience, they will feel encouraged to meet me halfway and do the same. As we move together toward vulnerability, potential will emerge for greater support, community, and intimacy between us.

Importantly, intimacy is dependent on the modes of communication at play between performers and audience members. An issue I question in my personal and professional life is how intimacy is transformed by technology, whether video, audio, lighting, web, medical devices, or more. If "seeing" one another deeply and vulnerably heightens closeness, then I can search for definitive ways in which technology enhances intimacy for me. For example, the camera can penetrate angles and surfaces of the body not visible in embodied relations. Yet, a common concern I hear from fellow dance artists regarding video documentations, adaptations, and incarnations of dance, is that they miss the presence of live bodies with their sweat, breath, weight, and warmth. In my own personal struggle for intimacy online in a long-distance relationship, I found that communicating with my partner on Skype intensified my awareness of the distance between us, and of our physical absence in one another's lives. At the same time, an internal dialogue urged me to consider that if I could not connect to my lover's virtual presence, how was I connecting to performers in recorded or live video? When I create dance for camera or integrate video projection in live dance performance, how do I foster intimacy between the performers and viewers?

For me, recorded video can increase the vulnerability and intimacy of a performance by exposing the body in unfamiliar ways via framing, angle, lighting, distance, context, and more. Projecting recorded video in performance offers portals into other sites and times to erect relationships between here and now with there and then. When I view a live video feed, however, I relate to the virtual image as a part of the current moment. Live streams create digital doubles of people and places in "real time." When I enter a live video feed such as a Skype transmission, my analog flesh is captured by a web cam, dematerialized into discrete digital data, streamed via the Internet, and finally (or simultaneously?), materializes on my partner's screen. We can interact in the present moment, in a shared and malleable site of reality. But is that *me* he's seeing? Am I really *there* with him, or am I *here* in my bedroom? Am I in two sites at once? Live video feeds complicate my perception of embodied presence and absence in time and space, transforming the way in which I experience intimacy in relationships on and off stage.

In *Gently between us* the dancers interacted simultaneously on stage and screen via real-time video feeds. The juxtaposition of live and virtual relationships raised questions for me regarding the character of embodied and mediated intimacy in life and performance. In an early section of *Gently between us*, the two male dancers, Erik and Quentin, stand in opposite corners of the stage, reaching forward for an imaginary partner. Each is locked in a narrow beam of light from the projector, which reveals and conceals their actions as the lights fade on and off. Gradually, they appear one at a time in the central projection screen, so that when we see Erik on stage he is joined by Quentin on screen, and vice versa. Cameras stand next to the men on stage to illustrate the immediate passage between the live action and video feed. Eventually, the men arrive together in the central screen, performing a virtual duet in which they pass in and out of one another's arms. Whereas they are isolated and apart on stage, they connect and relate to one another on screen. Here, technology mediates and makes possible a level of intimacy that is not being achieved in live interaction. The men's duet continues later on in the piece when Erik reaches his hands slowly in and out of a camera's eye. A live feed of Erik's hands is projected onto Quentin's bare stomach as he stands facing the audience downstage. At moments, Quentin presses into the image of Erik's hands on his stomach, imprinting the virtual touch into his skin. To this point in the work, Erik and Quentin have never made eye contact or connected physically. Their perceived relationship is mediated and materialized by the cameras, computer software, and projectors, existing solely in a virtual meeting place. Thus a significant turnabout occurs when Erik tentatively approaches Quentin, replacing the projected hands with real touch. In *Gently between us*, the cameras and projection expand the dancers' relationships with one another and the audience beyond live interaction to induce new experiences of vulnerability and intimacy in the realm of technology.

To create the above scene, I sourced from a vulnerable personal situation, which branched out to larger social and political concerns regarding mediated intimacy and embodiment/virtuality. Being able to connect my individual experience to other people and issues fostered understanding and intimacy between us. Moving with vulnerability in my dance projects via choreography, video, sound, and other media is at times uncomfortable, frightening, and frustrating, but I continue on this personal–communal–political path because I feel the journey heightens my level of connection with collaborators, audiences, and the world around me. I expose my soft spots and ask others to do the same lest we might "see" ourselves and one another intimately. On my path to creating dance, I arrive at moments in which I feel profoundly linked to certain people or places. I imagine I know and understand him/her/me/it. Just when I think I have captured who/what/where/why/how I am in one moment, the clock ticks on and variables change. So I dive back into my process and continue on a vulnerable and uncertain search for new moments of intimacy, on and off stage.

## 100 Drops of Uncertainty

No matter how deeply I invest in my creative process, no guarantee exists that people will like, or more importantly to me, feel moved and touched by what emerges. As a choreographer and performer I depend on my own and the audience's capacity for self-reflexivity, critical engagement, and empathy. In my experience, empathy is essential to building intimacy. My capacity to deeply *see* someone else relies on my empathic awareness and processing in mind and body of my own lived experiences. Furthermore, building intimacy with someone, momentary or lifelong, requires effort from both parties. I view communication in performance as a reciprocal process in which meaning emerges through the meeting of performers with audience. I confide that on occasions I have attended shows preoccupied with my own worries, sheepishly exhausted, or in such a rotten mood that the artists might as well be talking to a mannequin. When I fail to be receptive or generous as an audience member, I perceive little from a show. If I see the same piece in a more sensitive mood, perhaps I still will not be moved. But if I fail to try, I will never connect, and that is my loss as a spectator. I choose to share my vulnerability as a choreographer and performer with the hope that some audience members will risk doing the same, whether in personal reflection, with a friend, or with me. When watching dance or meeting a person for the first time, I try to shelve immediate value judgments that label him/her/it good or bad. Instead, I call on empathy lest we might move together toward sharing vulnerability, and eventually intimacy.

Might, I said. Admittedly, being vulnerable means risking rejection, hurt, and pain; this may or may not lead to intimacy. Participants from social worker Brené Brown's (2011) study described vulnerability in their lives as: "the willingness to say 'I love you' first, the willingness to do something where there are no guarantees, the willingness to breathe through waiting for the doctor to call after your mammogram." In my experience, fear of judgment impedes my own and my collaborators' potential for growth, connection, and discovery, because we are less willing to access and share what drives and directs us. Undoubtedly, occasions arise when restricting vulnerability is necessary and wise for self-protection and preservation, for example, in the absence of trust and support. In a performance situation, with a theater full of strangers, why would I choose to put myself on the line? In a crowd of 1,000 or even 100 spectators, inevitably not everyone will like or connect to my work. For me, accepting this reality and continuing to share anyway in order to bond with as many people as possible requires humility. Once in a while, I feel the sting of rejection, but the swelling and irritation soon subside.

My favorite moments in rehearsal are those when I feel embarrassed, uncomfortable, and unbalanced. Maybe favorite is the wrong word; they are my most productive and inspiring moments. I agree with theater director Ann Bogart (2001): "if what you do or make does not embarrass you sufficiently, then it is probably not personal or intimate enough" (p. 116). Leaving my embarrassment in the dark only helps the feeling breed. Moments of discomfort guide me toward my soft spots, which I gently unbandage to begin my own recovery, and help others do the same. I find the uncertainty that stems from self-exposure can be a generative force in creation, as long as trust and support are present equally. Moving in the direction of what I do not know; who I do not know; how I do not know; where I do not know; and why I do not know expands my inner and outer comprehension. By avoiding uncertainty, I stunt personal and professional growth. The character of research in contemporary dance is subjective, experiential, and qualitative, with outcomes that are not easily measured. My discoveries as a dance artist are liquid, moving, and uncertain, yet they have a concrete effect on the way I perceive myself, others, and the world.

A source of much uncertainty for me during the creation of *Gently between us* was the integration of multiple media with movement. The balancing of technical and creative concerns, codependent as they are, was a constant juggling act. Merging multiple mediums in performance is very time consuming, and at moments I simply wanted to be alone with the dancers in a studio. Instead, for many frustrating rehearsals I worked in the media lab with all of the elements developing side by side: movement, video, lights, and sound. I was trying to gain perspective on how the unique media were interacting, in order to guide detailed choices within each discipline. My focus had to zoom out, zoom in, zoom out, zoom in. Furthermore, the reality of having many strong voices in rehearsal—the dancers, media director, composer, rehearsal director, and occasional outside eyes—both offered support and pressure. I wanted to hear everyone, which resulted in difficulty hearing myself. I did a lot of reflective writing to gain perspective and connect to my vision for the piece. I spent hours lying in bed visualizing different possibilities, images, and movements. Through deciding what moments were most effective and important to me, I began a process of pruning that allowed the shape of the piece to be revealed.

Without a doubt, I could not have navigated my stormy uncertainty without clear communication and investment from collaborators. I worked closely with the media director, and we necessarily encountered moments of tension and conflict that, although they were difficult, deepened and strengthened the work by making the production something neither one of us could have created alone. In the words of Bogart: "Art is violent. To be decisive is violent" (p. 45). She elaborates by explaining: "Another kind of violence is the violence of disagreement. I believe that it is in disagreement that certain truths about the human condition are revealed. It is when images, ideas or people disagree that one senses the truth" (p. 55). Through sharing and negotiating at times divergent opinions or preferences, a creative process ensued that revealed solutions I had not yet imagined. Similarly, the dancers offered resounding support through their literal, emotional, and intellectual presence and reliability over time. I felt their commitment through patience, self-discipline, and perhaps most of all, moments of visible frustration and questioning within the project. Whenever they did not understand or feel connected to a part of the piece, they challenged themselves, one another, and me to keep searching and figuring the process out. I appreciate that they were not a complacent, passive cast, but rather articulate, proactive, and engaged in the physical, intellectual, and overall development of the work. I related to the dancers as collaborators, asking questions when I was lost, and incorporating their ideas and feedback. I also had valuable input from my advisors, the rehearsal director, and peers. The reality of creating an interdisciplinary piece is that I was truly reliant on the commitment and effort of an entire team. I had to hone my ability to ask for help, as I ventured into areas of great uncertainty.

Uncertainty revealed to me the ongoing negotiation in my creative process between moments when I can let go for the ride, versus those when I need to take the reins with strength and resistance. For me, dance is a process of problem solving in body and mind, in which each question or answer breeds 10-fold more. This can be overwhelming. As an antidote Bogart proclaims: "When in doubt, when you are lost, don't stop. Instead, concentrate on detail" (p. 135). Pick a detail and follow along as the path threads, fabricating material to clothe you in your vulnerable, intimate, and uncertain journey to creating dance.

## Combine and Mix Well

In the days leading up to the premiere of *Gently between us*, my anxiety mounted. Not because I worried that the performance was not "good" or that people would dislike the piece, but because I was struck that I might be questioned personally for the content of the piece. I anticipated that the audience would react to an overall sense of darkness and antagonism, as well as raw emotion, physicality, and sexuality in the work. Following the show, two of my dance students confided to me that they were frightened that this piece came out of me.

At a thank you brunch with the cast a week after the premiere, my dancers expressed unease with sluggish applause following the show each night. I too faced silence from some spectators. My initial reaction was insecurity. *They all hate it. But that's OK, right?* Gradually, individuals approached me to share how they connected to the work emotionally and intellectually. Some expressed a need for time to process the experience. I know others simply feel they failed to understand it or outright disliked it, and might never think about it again. Nonetheless, I found audience members more thoughtful, engaged, and inquisitive about this project than my past work. Their emotive, interpretive, and associative engagement with the material was satisfying and inspiring to me. Extended discussions with peers, mentors, and strangers reaffirmed my confidence in the worth of a personal, vulnerable process, which I view as the base for accessibility in dance. Audiences cannot enter a piece kinesthetically/emotionally/mentally if the creators keep their guards up during the process and performance. Social worker Brené Brown (2011) points out: "in order for connection to happen, we have to allow ourselves to be seen, really seen." I resonate with this statement vis-à-vis relationships between directors, performers, and spectators in dance. In my creations, I attempt to let the audience *see* me, and the performers, with vulnerability and intimacy.

When I serve up a dance, I can never help but feel that piece is not quite finished. I obsess over whether the work needs one more pinch of this, or another teaspoon of that. I need time to fully taste and digest my conception, letting go of what I anticipated to find when I popped my concoction out of the oven. I swallow one bite at a time, sweet, sour, or spicy, absorbing the results of my labor. Whether the guests will receive food poisoning or essential nutrition will not be evident in their bodies for some hours or days, but I eagerly observe the immediate feedback of their senses. Everyone's taste is different. Some ask for more meat, more veggies, more bread, more salt. Some are full after the first dish, whereas others leave hungry. Course by course, I ingest information that inspires me to question, revise, and transform my creative process in future creations. In *Gently between us*, as in all my projects, the combination of vulnerability, intimacy, and uncertainty formed a batter from which I baked a performance that I find to be healthy and satisfying. I hope that the piece will nourish others as well.

## References

Bogart, A. (2001). *A director prepares: Seven essays on art and theatre.* New York: Routledge.

Brown, B. (2011, August 10). The power of vulnerability. [Video Webcast]. *TED Talks.* Retrieved from http://www.ted.com/talks/brene_brown_on_vulnerability.html.

## Epilogue

# Into the Light

### Edward C. Warburton

As I ascend to the dance studio, I try to relax. Remember, I remind myself, this is just his first-ever *informal* showing, not a full-scale performance at the Metropolitan Opera House in New York City! If my sometimes overly exuberant child decides to do something unplanned and unrehearsed, like running around yelling at the top of his voice, I remind myself, "It's no big deal." Like many dancers I know, I am a naturally shy person offstage, so the prospect of my child disrupting an event, any event, always worries me. Over the past few years, I have learned that impulsive behavior comes naturally to little ones: Anything can happen at anytime and probably will. No big deal. "Stay calm," I mutter to myself unconvinced, as a smiling parent looks sideways at my tense demeanor. Out of habit, I slip off my shoes before entering the dance studio. A familiar disorientation sweeps over me. The rituals and routines, look and feel of dance class are second nature, and yet the spirits and spaces, attitudes and beliefs that animate dance are unique to each and every place. I sit down quickly and survey the scene.

Thirteen dancers aged 4 to 6 years old sit in a rough line, facing front, giggly and fidgety. I glance nervously at my son, Haydn, not wanting to distract him or call attention to myself. I do not want to take him out of the moment (or the line!). He scans the room, long blond curls trailing behind. When he spies me, I smile. He grins, eyes wide. His shoulders lift up in a delighted fashion as if to say, "Look at me!" He is hard to miss. He is the only boy, the only child in blue shorts and tee shirt in a sea of pink leotards, tights, and tutus. A lot of ink has been spilled over the lack of

American boys in dance and so, although Haydn's singular position in the class does not surprise me, I do not celebrate the absence of other boys. I sense trepidation in his delight and my body responds in kind. So cute, but . . . my doubts are interrupted by the young dance teacher who sings out, "Ready to dance! Ready to show our dance?" The children respond with eager cries, and everyone in the room smiles. The teacher is a former student of mine and I am feeling doubly proud today. When she sees me, she smiles and raises her shoulders in a delighted fashion as if to say, "Look at us!" The class begins with a brief warm-up: bending and stretching and rising and sinking and turning and traveling. With surprisingly few disruptions, the dancers perform the short routine. They welcome the invitation to improvise in solos and duets. They end in a circle, bow left and right. Showing over. The appreciative applause acts as release valve, sending the children into the arms of their enamored parents.

Driving home, I wonder silently about my tepid response to this happy event. Am I so jaded by a life in dance—an uncertain journey balanced precariously between trepidation and delight—that I am unable to revel in the innocent joy of children dancing to the *Lion King*? Creating dance in America requires one to develop an unambiguous resilience against popular norms and cultural expectations. Has resilience evolved into resistance to creating dance for my son, for others? I have been lucky and privileged in my pursuit. From the time I left home for high school at the North Carolina School of the Arts to a professional ballet career to teaching dance in higher education, I stayed in the field. I owe more to my parents, teachers, and mentors than I can ever possibly repay. But, more often than not, the road was rough and precarious with too many off-ramps, not at all the paved highways and freeways that I had imagined. The destinations were never clearly demarcated. I drew the map after the fact. I struggled to maintain a moving identity: a grounded, thriving, dancing self. Do I want that for my son, for anyone? What value does dance add to a life?

I recall a time long before my son's birth when I began serious investigation of this question. I was at the tail end of my performing career. Injured and introspective at 28 years old, I trembled at the prospect of a financially insecure and uncertain professional future. One day I opened a letter from my mother, a long-time educator, and out fell a bizarre sounding article on something called "Project Zero." Founded by philosopher Nelson Goodman in the mid-1960s at Harvard University, this highly idiosyncratic research group set out to unravel the nature of artistic thinking: to assert the cognitive value of a creative life. Noting that next to nothing was known about this topic, Goodman dubbed the group "Project Zero." I sat and thought for a moment and then the penny dropped: the value of an examined life in art. And thus began an abiding interest in dance cognition and creativity, beginning as a member of Project Zero, deepened while studying for a doctorate in human development and psychology, and continued to the present.

At first, I focused on the arts and human development, examining early learning in dance and the development of movement expression. Later, I turned to the creative process of professional dancers as performing artists. To aid my investigation, I traveled as a research fellow in summer 2007 to Jacob's Pillow Dance, originally founded by modern dance pioneer Ted Shawn in 1942. The Jacob's Pillow Archives—specifically the Pillow Talk series and post-performance audiotapes and performance videos—were essential to my investigation. The Pillow research residency gave me access to an extraordinarily rich and diverse archive that exists only in Becket, Massachusetts; one that included both actual performances of specific works and records of dancers' thoughts about performing them. This research was only the first step in the investigative process, but a crucial one. I began to listen closely to the voices and experiences of a diverse group of performers immersed in the creative act of dancing. For me, the seeds of *Creating Dance* began then and there.

I quickly learned that to undertake the study of performing artists is to confront a paradox. Across the globe, public interest in performing artists is enormous, yet careful study of such individuals and groups on the part of psychologists and social scientists is exceedingly limited. The research literature from the 1950s shows a surge of interest in creativity. However, the vast majority of research is based on small samples of distinguished scientists and elite artists, largely in music (composers) and the visual arts (painters). More recently, an increased interest in the study of dance and creativity has emerged (Press & Warburton, 2007). A number of projects have focused on individual choreographers, but the voices of dancers, teachers, and administrators—all those who make possible the work itself—were missing from these investigations. When one considers the *process* of creating dance, one must appreciate the types and stages of creativity, the social influences, and environments that undermine or enhance creativity, and the relationship between people, identity, and the dance. In other words, to appreciate what makes any person or artistic work creative, one must take a systemic approach. One must consider the whole of creating dance. One must learn not only from those who achieve fame and recognition but also hear from those who, through determined exertion and profound passion, create a life rich in dance for themselves and others.

We arrive home. I unbuckle Haydn from the car seat and, unconstrained by his father's ruminations, he bounds out of the car calling, "Daddy, look!" Out of the corner of my eye, I catch a bending-stretching-rising-turning-traveling-leaping son. I am momentarily blinded, tears spring to my eyes. In the blur, *Creating Dance* fills my mind. Words and images flood in from nine different conversations of trepidation and delight. I hear a glorious cacophony of nine stories of love and struggle that resolve into a single extraordinary tale of total connection in life and art. My body begins to release. Finally, I relax. I bend, stretch, rise, and turn to follow my beautiful boy taking flight into the light.

## Reference

Press, C., & Warburton, E. C. (2007). Creativity research in dance. In L. Bresler (Ed.), *International handbook of research in arts education* (pp. 1271-1286). New York: Kluwer/Springer.

# About the Editors

**Carol M. Press**, Ed.D., received her doctorate in Interdisciplinary Studies between Dance and Clinical Psychology from Columbia Teachers College. Her book, *The Dancing Self: Creativity, Modern Dance, Self Psychology and Transformative Education* (Hampton Press, 2002), engages the relational dynamics between dance, creativity, dance history, aesthetics, psychology, pedagogy, and the vital exchanges between sense of self, community and culture. She is published nationally and internationally in such volumes and journals as *Psychoanalytic Inquiry*, the *Annals of the New York Academy of Sciences*, *International Handbook of Arts Education* (co-authored with Dr. Warburton), *Journal of the American Academy of Psychoanalysis and Dynamic Psychiatry*, *Zeitschrift Fur Tanztherapie* (*Journal for Dance Therapy*), and *Selbstpsychologie: Europaische Zeitschrift Fur Psychoanalytische Therapie Und Forschung* (*Self Psychology: European Journal for Psychoanalytic Therapy and Research*). Dr. Press's dance-making provides the foundation for her scholarship, and frequently she presents them together at conferences. Most recently she was invited by the Società Psicoanalitica Italiana (Italian Psychoanalytic Society) to present a paper and perform her choreography at the Spoleto Arts Festival, July 2012, in Spoleto, Italy, as part of L'enigma della creatività nell'Arte (The Enigma of Creativity in Art). She was key personnel for the National Dance Education Organization, developing their Research Database. Dr. Press teaches dance academics at the University of California, Santa Barbara. All of her teaching, art-making, and scholarship concentrate on deepening exploration through interdisciplinary discovery and significant exchange between action and theory.

**Edward C. (Ted) Warburton,** Ed.D., is Associate Professor of Dance at the University of California, Santa Cruz. He received early training at the North Carolina School of the Arts and danced professionally with American Ballet Theater II, Houston Ballet and Boston Ballet. His interdisciplinary interests in dance cognition, creativity, and technology stem from graduate work at Harvard University where he completed a doctorate in human development and psychology. A widely published author, his research examines the relational practices and processes that enhance (or undermine) dancers' abilities to convey the intention and feeling of the works they perform. He is currently a member of the international performance and research project *ArtsCross*: a multi-year initiative to study transcultural dance-making and choreographic process in Asia and Europe. His creative works explore the ways performative technologies extend theatrical artists' dramatic range across multiple media, people, places, spaces and time zones. His performance projects and writings on dance and technology have received critical recognition from the *New York Times* and have been showcased on the cover of *Leonardo*, the journal of the International Society for the Arts, Sciences and Technology. His work has enjoyed the support of generous granting organizations and institutions, including Beijing Dance Academy, Dance New Amsterdam, Jacob's Pillow Dance, National Endowment of the Arts, National Science Foundation, New York University, ResCen Research Centre at Middlesex University, and the University of California.

# About the Contributors

**Bill Evans**, M.F.A., C.M.A., has uniquely woven his work as a professional choreographer and performer with a career in dance education. Since 2004 he has served as visiting professor/guest artist in the Department of Dance at The College at Brockport, State University of New York. Between 1967 and 2004, he was based at four state universities: the University of Utah (choreographer/dancer/artistic coordinator with Repertory Dance Theatre and assistant professor in Department of Modern Dance); the University of Washington (his professional Bill Evans Dance Company [BEDCO] was in residence and he served as visiting professor of dance); Indiana University (BEDCO was in residence and he served as associate professor and director of contemporary dance); the University of New Mexico (BEDCO was in residence and he served as full professor and head of dance). He has been awarded a Guggenheim Fellowship, an honorary doctorate of fine arts from Cornish College of the Arts in Seattle, the National Dance Education Organization Lifetime Achievement Award, the New Mexico Governor's Award for Achievement and Excellence in the Arts, and numerous grants and fellowships from the National Endowment for the Arts. Since 1999, he has conducted the Bill Evans Summer Dance Teachers' Intensive Workshop and Certification Program in the Evans Laban-Based Modern Dance Technique.

**Catherine Turocy**, B.F.A., today's leading choreographer/reconstructor in the field of 18th-century dance with over 60 Baroque operas to her credit, has been decorated by the French Republic as a Chevalier in the Order of Arts and Letters. She received the prestigious Bessie Award in New York City for Sustained Achievement in Choreography as well as the Natalie Skelton Award for Artistic Excellence. In 1980 she received the Dance Film Association Award for *The Art of Dancing*. In 1979 Turocy and Ann Jacoby founded The New York Baroque Dance Company (NYBDC) which Ms. Turocy directs today. The NYBDC specializes in 17th- and 18th-century programs ranging from street performances to fully staged operas and has toured North America, Europe and Japan with conductors James Richman, John Eliot Gardiner, Christopher Hogwood, and Nicholas McGegan. Ms. Turocy graduated with a BFA in Dance from The Ohio State University. She is a founding member of the Society of Dance History Scholars and was the Ad Interim Chair of Dance in 1995-96 at Southern Methodist University. Currently she is a visiting faculty member at the Juilliard School in New York City.

**Christopher Pilafian** graduated from Interlochen Arts Academy and attended Juilliard, where he was awarded the Doris Humphrey Scholarship and the Louis Horst Fellowship. He became a founding member, principal dancer and Associate Artistic Director of Jennifer Muller/The Works, performing in eleven NYC seasons and throughout Europe, the Middle East, and North, Central and South America from 1974 to 1989. He has created over 45 dance works including commissions for Princeton University, Dance Kaleidoscope, Jennifer Muller/The Works, Repertory-West Dance Company, American Repertory Dance Company, San Diego Dance Theater and Santa Barbara Dance Theatre. A member of the dance faculty at University of California, Santa Barbara since 1990, Mr. Pilafian accepted, in 2011, the positions of Vice Chair of the Department of Theater and Dance, Director of Dance, and Artistic Director of Santa Barbara Dance Theater. He is also a visual artist.

**Darwin Prioleau**, Ph.D., is the Dean of the School of The Arts, Humanities and Social Science, and a professor of dance, at The College at Brockport, State University of New York. Her professional career spans over twelve years in New York City and France dancing with various dance companies, including soloist with The Nat Horne Company, Contemporary Dance Spectrum and Ed Kresley Dance Company, and featured dancer in several off-Broadway musicals. Dr. Prioleau has worked intensively with such dance masters as Alvin Ailey, Jimmy Truitte, Matt Mattox and Rosella Hightower. She has been a free-lance modern and jazz dance choreographer and master teacher in the Ohio, Massachusetts, New York, Missouri and European professional dance communities. Her areas of expertise include jazz dance, modern dance, pedagogy and choreography. Nationally, Dr. Prioleau is actively involved in arts education advocacy and has published articles in *Journal of Dance Education* and *Arts Education Policy*. She has presented papers on "Leadership of the Arts in Higher Education" at various national conferences. In addition, she is the recipient of the NDEO 2006 Outstanding Leadership Award. Presently, she is the President of the National Dance Education Organization.

**David Leventhal**, B.A., is a founding teacher and Program Manager for Dance for PD®, a collaborative program of the Mark Morris Dance Group and Brooklyn Parkinson Group that has now been used as a model for classes in more than 60 communities in seven countries. He leads classes for people with Parkinson's disease around the world and trains other teachers in the Dance for PD® approach. He has written about the program for such publications as *Dance Gazette* and *Room 217*, and has a chapter in a forthcoming book called *Moving Ideas: Multimodal Learning in Communities and Schools* (Lexington Books). A frequent guest speaker at Parkinson's conferences and symposiums, he serves on the Board of Directors for the Society for the Arts in Healthcare. He danced with the Mark Morris Dance Group from 1997-2011, performing principal roles in Morris' *The Hard Nut*, *L'Allegro, il Penseroso ed il Moderato*, and *Romeo and Juliet, on Motifs of Shakespeare*. He is on the faculty of the Mark Morris Dance Center in Brooklyn. He received a 2010 New York Dance and Performance Award (BESSIE) for sustained achievement in the work of Mark Morris. Mr. Leventhal received a B.A. with honors from Brown University.

**John-Mario Sevilla**, B.A. (University of Hawai'i at Mānoa), M.A. (Teachers College, Columbia University), M.F.A. (University of Wisconsin-Milwaukee), is the Director of the 92Y Harkness Dance Center, former Director of the Dance Education Laboratory, and adjunct professor at the New York University Steinhardt School of Culture, Education, and Human Development. He currently teaches modern dance and assessment in dance education. He studies hula with Kumu Hula Hōkūlani Holt. He has written for the *Journal of Dance Education* and created curricula for New York City Ballet and 92nd Street Y and numerous assessment items for New York State and City. A former Director of Education at New York City Ballet and dance captain for Pilobolus, he has also danced for choreographers Joseph Mills, Rebecca Stenn, Susan Koff, Daman Harun, Kimani Fowlin, Erin Dudley, Lisa Giobbi, Nikolais and Louis, Shapiro and Smith, Janis Brenner, Anna Sokolow and Bill Cratty, juggler Michael Moschen, animator Laura Margulies, drag artist Sherry Vine, poet John Unterecker and Dine sand painter/healer Walking Thunder. His choreography has appeared at La MaMa, Judson Church, Dance Theater Workshop, 92Y Tribeca, Columbia University, ABC No Rio, Lower East Side Tenement Museum, The Asia Society and Bronx Academy of Art and Dance.

**Linda Caldwell**, Ph.D. and Certified Movement Analyst in Laban Movement Studies, is professor and coordinator of the low-residential, dance doctoral program at Texas Woman's University. She serves as the co-chair for Research and Documentation for the World Dance Alliance-Americas and in this capacity will be editing the WDA-A newsletter in the future. Her current interests include discovering how to engage action and the dancer's voice into scholarly writing and pedagogical methods for creating "risky readings" about dance practice. She is also working as a consultant for dance programs developing quality online course work in the university setting. Her dissertation and past publications concern a 15-year exchange with Poland's contemporary dance company, The Silesian Dance Theatre. Dr. Caldwell's choreography has been performed in dance festivals in Lyons, France and Krakow, Poland, as well as chosen twice for the National College Dance Festivals in Washington, D.C. and Tempe, Arizona.

**Melanie Ríos Glaser**, B.F.A, is Artistic Director and Co-CEO of The Wooden Floor in Santa Ana, California. Born and raised in Guatemala, she received her BFA from the Juilliard School, was named a Kennedy Center Fellow in 1998, and a Fulbright Scholar in Paris in 2003. Melanie has choreographed more than 30 pieces for groups that include the Department of Dance at the University of California, Irvine (UCI), Group Motion Dance Theatre Company, Ballet Moderno y Folklórico de Guatemala, Ballet de Cali, her own Mosquito Dance Company and The Wooden Floor among others. Her work has been performed in Mexico, Guatemala, El Salvador, Nicaragua, Costa Rica, Panama, France, Colombia, Brazil, California, Philadelphia, New York, and elsewhere. As a movement artist for over seventeen years, Melanie has a marked interest in dance improvisation, contact improvisation and dance composition. She was certified in 2003 as a somatic educator at Moving on Center in Oakland, California. She often guest teaches at universities such as the University of the Arts in Philadelphia and, most recently, at UCI. She enjoys writing about dance for youth development, current trends and acting as curator of live performance. She also volunteers as a consultant for other nonprofits on issues of nonprofit management, governance, fundraising, and programming.

**Teoma Naccarato**, M.F.A., completed her degree in Dance at The Ohio State University in 2011 with a concentration in Choreography and Dance Technology. Her research focuses on the interplay of creative practice with theory, harnessing dance and multi-media to facilitate personal and social awareness and growth. Naccarato received her BFA in Contemporary Dance from Concordia University in 2004, and spent several years as an independent dancer, dance teacher and choreographer in Montreal. In 2005 she founded Naccarato Dance, presenting work at festivals across Canada, the United States, and South America. In 2007, Naccarato co-founded a dance film organization with filmmaker Desh Fernando titled Nacando Productions for which she choreographed, directed and edited numerous video dance projects. Naccarato has performed nationally and internationally with choreographers Michael Montanaro, Marianne Desjardins, Catherine Castonguay, Ilona Dougherty, and others. In Autumn 2011, she was a visiting lecturer in the Department of Dance at the Ohio State University, and the interdisciplinary production manager for the Experimental Media and Movement Arts Lab (EMMA). In Spring 2012, she served as a visiting professor at Florida State University, teaching courses in dance composition, technique and mediated performance. For information on past, present and upcoming projects visit www.naccarato.org/dance.

# Author/Subject Index